THE LAYMAN'S BIBLE COMMENTARY

THE LAYMAN'S BIBLE COMMENTARY
IN TWENTY-FIVE VOLUMES

THE LAYMAN'S
BIBLE COMMENTARY

Balmer H. Kelly, *Editor*

Donald G. Miller   *Associate Editors*   Arnold B. Rhodes

Dwight M. Chalmers, *Editor, John Knox Press*

VOLUME 20

THE

ACTS OF THE APOSTLES

Albert C. Winn

JOHN KNOX PRESS

ATLANTA

10 9 8 7 6 5 4 3 2

Complete set: ISBN: 0-8042-3086-2
This volume: 0-8042-3080-3
Library of Congress Card Number: 59-10454
First paperback edition 1982
Printed in the United States of America
John Knox Press
Atlanta, Georgia 30365

PREFACE

The LAYMAN'S BIBLE COMMENTARY is based on the conviction that the Bible has the Word of good news for the whole world. The Bible is not the property of a special group. It is not even the property and concern of the Church alone. It is given to the Church for its own life but also to bring God's offer of life to all mankind —wherever there are ears to hear and hearts to respond.

It is this point of view which binds the separate parts of the LAYMAN'S BIBLE COMMENTARY into a unity. There are many volumes and many writers, coming from varied backgrounds, as is the case with the Bible itself. But also as with the Bible there is a unity of purpose and of faith. The purpose is to clarify the situations and language of the Bible that it may be more and more fully understood. The faith is that in the Bible there is essentially one Word, one message of salvation, one gospel.

The LAYMAN'S BIBLE COMMENTARY is designed to be a concise non-technical guide for the layman in personal study of his own Bible. Therefore, no biblical text is printed along with the comment upon it. This commentary will have done its work precisely to the degree in which it moves its readers to take up the Bible for themselves.

The writers have used the Revised Standard Version of the Bible as their basic text. Occasionally they have differed from this translation. Where this is the case they have given their reasons. In the main, no attempt has been made either to justify the wording of the Revised Standard Version or to compare it with other translations.

The objective in this commentary is to provide the most helpful explanation of fundamental matters in simple, up-to-date terms. Exhaustive treatment of subjects has not been undertaken.

In our age knowledge of the Bible is perilously low. At the same time there are signs that many people are longing for help in getting such knowledge. Knowledge of and about the Bible is, of course, not enough. The grace of God and the work of the Holy Spirit are essential to the renewal of life through the Scriptures. It is in the happy confidence that the great hunger for the Word is a sign of God's grace already operating within men, and that the Spirit works most wonderfully where the Word is familiarly known, that this commentary has been written and published.

THE EDITORS AND
THE PUBLISHERS

INTRODUCTION

The Unity of Luke-Acts

A Remarkable Two-Volume Work

Before the end of the first century, two remarkable documents were circulating within the Christian fellowship. Taken together they must have comprised the longest piece of writing the Church had produced—so long that it made two "books." Each volume filled a complete roll of papyrus, about 32 feet long, when copied out carefully by hand. It was easy to recognize that these were two halves of a single work, for the second roll took up where the first had left off, and both were dedicated to a man named Theophilus. The author's name never appeared on the rolls themselves. It may have been attached to the first copies on a little, separate "tag." If so, it was soon lost. So the two-volume work circulated anonymously.

This remarkable document told the story of the beginnings of the Christian Church, from the day the angel promised the birth of John the Baptist until the gospel was freely preached in Rome by the Apostle Paul. In two brief pamphlets—they are hardly long enough for modern readers to call them "books"—the writer attempted to cover almost seventy years of history, and to explain the greatest events that ever happened. What a difficult task! Yet, in the judgment of the Early Church, the writer scored a brilliant success. Many scribes were willing to undertake the painstaking labor of making copies by hand. Soon Christians were reading this unique story of the birth of the Church wherever the Church had spread.

The Separation of the Two Books

Then something happened which separated the two rolls so that they began to be read, not as halves of a single work, but as two completely independent books. Fortunately, the writer had done his work so competently that each half could stand independently very well. Yet many, many readers have missed the rich understanding which the whole work was designed to give, because ever since the second century they have usually read only one half at a time.

It is easy to understand what happened. The first roll contained the story of Jesus' deeds and teachings while he was here in the flesh. The second roll contained the continuation of his deeds and teachings through the Church. As these rolls circulated among the Christians, the first roll gradually was grouped with other records of the ministry of Jesus. Soon four such records were accepted as authoritative. They were collected together and called "the Gospel." Tradition suggested the names of writers for these four Gospels, and the first roll of our document became known as "the Gospel according to Luke." The second roll, left by itself, eventually became known as "the Acts of the Apostles."

The separation of the two rolls has lasted down to our own day. Since the Gospel according to John is always printed between Luke and Acts in our Bibles, most of us fail to realize that these are two halves of a single work. Even those who are aware of it never quite overcome the impression that we have here two independent books which happen to be by the same writer. We do not even have a name for the single work, and have had to invent the awkward expression "Luke-Acts."

The Author

The author of Luke-Acts was the principal contributor to the New Testament. He wrote one-fourth of its contents—more, even, than Paul, with all his letters. Such a voluminous writer would normally leave some hints about himself in his work. But this author has lost himself so completely in the story he is telling that he drops only one important clue. That clue is the famous "we-passages."

The "We-Passages"

At Acts 16:10, while recording one of the missionary journeys of Paul, the writer very abruptly, without any explanation, begins to use the first person plural: "And when he had seen the vision, immediately *we* sought to go into Macedonia." Just as abruptly, after verse 17 of the same chapter, the "we" disappears. Suddenly at 20:5, the first person plural appears again and continues to 21:18. Once again, in 27:1—28:16, the "we" is constant. The natural impression of these passages is that the writer was a companion of Paul during these particular periods of his life.

Did the Writer Know Paul?

But could the writer of Luke-Acts actually have been a companion of Paul? It is on this question that the real debate about the authorship of Luke-Acts has hinged for the past one hundred years. Some earnest and intelligent scholars have felt that the picture of Paul which we gain from his letters is very different from the picture of Paul which Acts gives. They say that a man who really knew the Paul who wrote the letters could never have written Acts. They point out that Paul's letters tell of journeys, incidents, and conflicts about which Acts says nothing. They interpret Paul's letters, especially Galatians, to show him completely independent of the Apostles at Jerusalem, and fiercely opposed to any observance of the Law of Moses by Christians. Could such a man really have agreed to the compromise recorded in Acts 15, or have circumcised Timothy (Acts 16:3), or have borne expenses for a Jewish vow (Acts 21:23-26), or have defended himself as a Pharisee (Acts 23:6)? Is it not more likely that the writer of Acts did not really know Paul?

Anyone who has studied Galatians carefully and who has tried to compare Galatians 2 with Acts 15 must take these objections very seriously. It is not easy to reconcile the Paul of the letters with the Paul of Acts. Yet we must realize that no man is altogether consistent, certainly not a volcanic personality like Paul. By his own admission, he strove to be all things to all men. "To the Jews I became as a Jew, in order to win Jews; to those under the law I became as one under the law—though not being myself under the law—that I might win those under the law" (I Cor. 9:20; see also vss. 19, 21-23). Here the Paul of the letters seems just as willing to compromise as does the Paul of Acts. We must face the fact that we possess only a fragment of Paul's correspondence, and that Acts itself relates only a few selected incidents from his life. We are trying to match two exceedingly fragmentary pictures. Who can say positively that if we had the whole picture in each case, the pictures would be contradictory?

If the writer did not know Paul, he has either imagined the "we-passages," or has copied them from a travel diary he found somewhere. Scholars who have excavated and studied the ancient Near East find it hard to believe that the "we-passages" are works of imagination. They fit too closely the geography, the politics, and the general customs of the era. Other interpreters who are experts in language are convinced that the rest of the book is in the same style as the "we-passages." One writer, they say, wrote it all.

The balance of the evidence would seem to support the natural impression given by the "we-passages." The writer of Luke-Acts was a companion of Paul. There are unsolved difficulties in this position. But there are much greater difficulties in any other explanation of the "we-passages."

Was the Writer Luke?

Once we assume that the writer of Luke-Acts was a companion of Paul, there is no reason to reject the familiar tradition that his name was Luke.

From the time when the first roll was grouped with the other Gospels, the unanimous and unbroken tradition of the Church was that our third Gospel and Acts were written by a man named Luke. Luke is referred to in Colossians 4:14; II Timothy 4:11; and Philemon 24. From these scanty references we learn that Luke was a Gentile (not "of the circumcision"; see Col. 4:11), a physician, and a companion of Paul during his imprisonment. This is all that is certainly known of him. It seems hardly likely that second-century Christians would have "selected" such an obscure man to name as the author of one-fourth of the New Testament. It is much more probable that they named him as the author because even then the tradition was strong and unanimous.

Without claiming to have solved all the difficulties, we will hereafter refer to the writer of Acts as Luke.

The Date

The last sentence of Acts is our main clue for dating Luke-Acts: "And he lived there two whole years . . ." Luke gives enough cross references to Roman history for us to date Paul's arrival at Rome somewhere between A.D. 57 and 62. When Acts was written, Paul had preached the gospel in Rome for two whole years. Therefore, Luke-Acts could not possibly have been completed before A.D. 59-64.

To date the book any more closely than that requires considerable guesswork. Does Acts end without telling of Paul's death because Paul was still in Rome when Luke wrote? If so, then we would take the earliest possible date. Does Luke hint that the fall of Jerusalem to the Roman army had already taken place when he wrote? Then we would date the book after A.D. 70. Does he at times quote from the writings of Josephus (a famous Jewish historian who wrote after A.D. 90)? This would mean that the book was not written before the very end of the first century. A companion of Paul would have been an old man by then. There is no compelling evidence on any of these points. Until better clues have been found, all we can say positively is that the writing of the book falls somewhere within the last forty years of the first century.

The Importance of Acts

Luke's second volume has in some ways turned out to be more important than his first. We would be immeasurably poorer if we did not have the Gospel according to Luke. We would lack the shepherds and the angel choir at Christmas, the Good Samaritan, the Prodigal Son, and other treasures too many to name. But we would have the most essential information about Jesus' life still preserved in Matthew, Mark, and John. On the other hand, if Acts were missing, we would grope in a fog of uncertainty and confusion about the origin of the Church. There is no other record.

Indeed, if Acts had not been written, we might have no New Testament. It seems probable that the publication of Luke-Acts and its wide reading by the Church prompted the collection of Paul's letters. They had been written before Luke-Acts and were treasured by local churches. But their collection and publication to the whole Church seems to have followed the publication of Acts. Later, the other apostolic writings were also collected because of the interest Acts had created. Acts is thus the link between the Gospels and the Letters. Without it, the New Testament might never have been formed.

The Purpose of Acts

Almost everyone who studies Acts agrees that the writer had a very definite purpose. The marks of it are everywhere. But not all agree on what that purpose was. This makes the book especially fascinating to all amateur detectives and lovers of mysteries.

The Statement in Luke 1:1-4

Has Luke himself left any statement about what he had in mind? As long as we confine ourselves to Acts alone, the answer is No. But if we remember what was said above about the unity of Luke-Acts, we will look for a statement at the beginning of the whole two-volume work. We will not be disappointed, for in Luke 1:1-4 there is a compact preface which sheds much light on our problem.

Luke begins by saying that he is not doing anything unique or unheard of. Many others have attempted the same task: "to compile a narrative of the things which have been accomplished among us." The "us" probably means here, as often in the New Testament, the Christian Church. Within the Church certain things have been "accomplished" (or "fulfilled"). This is a theological word. In certain events, says Luke, we have seen the fulfillment of God's purpose, particularly as that purpose is set down in Scripture. It is these special events which Luke is seeking to organize into an orderly account.

A Theological Purpose

But why, when other accounts of these special events existed, did Luke take pen in hand to write this particular two-volume work? Because a man named Theophilus and many others needed to "know the truth" (Luke 1:4) concerning the things of which they had been informed. In other words, Luke's readers had a general knowledge of the facts. What they needed was a proper theological understanding of them. The word "truth" (or "certainty") seems to imply that Luke's readers were uncertain. Their faith had been shaken. Something was casting doubt on whether the things that had happened really were fulfillments of God's purpose.

We wish the preface were more definite about Theophilus' problem. But this much seems clear. Luke is telling his story—both volumes of it—with a theological purpose. He is trying to help his fellow Christians get the right understanding of what had taken place in their midst. Luke-Acts is not, then, "history" in the modern sense of the word. It is not a complete and objective record of the period. It is a selected and interpreted record. Neither is Luke-Acts a defense of Christianity to some heathen official, or a brief for Paul's trial. Like all the other books of the New Testament, it is written by a Christian for Christians. It speaks from faith to faith.

The Shift from Jew to Gentile

For additional light on Theophilus' problem, we must turn to the body of Luke's two-volume work. We must notice what he selects to tell out of all he could have told. We must observe what he lifts out for special emphasis. Here the second volume seems to be more revealing than the first. We cannot be positive that we are reading the clues rightly, but we can suggest at least a possible answer.

There seems to be a tremendous emphasis in Acts on the change-over from a Church that was mainly a little sect within the Jewish nation to a Church scattered over the Roman Empire and largely Gentile in membership. Thus Acts begins in Jerusalem, the world center of Judaism, and ends in Rome, the world center of the Gentiles. More and more as the book progresses, the Jews reject the gospel and the Gentiles accept it. Four times, Paul turns from the Jews to the Gentiles (13:44-47; 18:5-7; 19: 8-9; 28:23-28). The last turning, at Rome, is the climax with which the book ends.

It is a fact of history that such a change-over took place in the first century. For those who lived through it, it created a serious theological problem. Remember that the only Bible the early Christians had was the Old Testament. Did not that Bible state that Israel was God's Chosen People, that he had made a Covenant with Israel, that he would send the Messiah to Israel? Now the Messiah had come and Israel had rejected him. Even after his resurrection, the Jews still would not accept him. And the Gentiles, to whom no promises had been made, with whom God had no Covenant, were pressing into the Church! Had the word of God failed? Had God rejected his people? Had his eternal purpose been thwarted? Such may have been Theophilus' problem.

At any rate, it is one of Luke's purposes to show that the rejection of the gospel by the Jews and its acceptance by the Gentiles is not an unexpected catastrophe. It is part of God's eternal purpose. God still has his Chosen People. But that people is now the Church, the true Israel, in which Gentiles have equal rights with Jews. Luke shows that the Scriptures anticipated this shift. In the Gospel he shows that Jesus, even during his ministry, had a special sympathy for non-Jews. And in Acts he shows the Holy Spirit blocking, guiding, driving the Church into this new understanding of itself.

If a modern historian could have recorded the history of the Early Church, he would doubtless have included much that Luke leaves out. But would he have grasped the essential issues as clearly? And would his book be as useful to us? After all, our interest in the Early Church is primarily theological, too. We want to understand what the Church is and how it fits into God's eternal purpose. Acts gives us the answer.

The Literary Form

Luke's Greek Style

Luke writes some of the best Greek in the New Testament. Only the writer of Hebrews can be compared with him in this respect. Other New Testament writers probably spoke and thought in Aramaic. Aramaic was closely akin to Hebrew and was the common language of Palestine in Jesus' day. But Luke's native tongue was Greek, and he had a "feel" for it.

Luke was not, however, a "literary" writer. He does not often use the classical Greek which people who wrote "bookish" books used. Most of his writing is in the common Greek of the street and the market place, the Greek that ordinary people understood. When he quotes Greek literature, it is only the familiar sayings that had passed into common use. In fact, the only book we can be sure he had read is the Septuagint, the Old Testament in its Greek translation.

The Septuagint affected him profoundly and colored his whole style. Just as the language of the English Bible formed the style of John Bunyan in *Pilgrim's Progress,* so the language of the Greek Bible formed Luke's style in Luke-Acts. When Luke is dealing with a Jewish situation, as in the infancy stories of the Gospel or the first half of Acts, his language is like the Septuagint. When he moves out into the Greek world in the last half of Acts, his language is more like the ordinary Greek of his day. Some interpreters think Luke's style varies because at times he is translating some Aramaic documents. Others are not convinced of this. But in any case, he can vary his style to suit his material. And he does this with the sensitivity of a real artist.

Selectivity

The very nature of his task forced Luke to be selective. When he set out to cover, on two papyrus rolls, Jesus' life and the first thirty years of church history, it is obvious that he had to omit far more than he included.

Again and again we find Luke summarizing a whole period in a brief, compact paragraph then selecting some one incident which is typical of that period and telling it in some detail. This rhythm of a general statement followed by a particular story is seen most clearly in the first twelve chapters of Acts.

Local Color

When he comes to the missionary work of Paul in the Greek-speaking cities around the Mediterranean, Luke is completely at home. He uses accurate titles for the local officials, he understands the complex political relationships within the Roman Empire, he treats local religions and customs with a sure hand. This gives his book the flavor and color of first-century life.

Interest

The details of Luke's style are not nearly so important as his over-all result. He has created one of the most interesting works of all time. The French writer Renan called Luke's Gospel the most beautiful book ever written. The theme of Luke's second volume does not lend itself as well to beauty; we might be closer to the mark to call Acts the most exciting book ever written.

Where else in one short pamphlet can we find so much that is thrilling and moving? From one end of the book to the other, crowds are rushing to some point of feverish excitement: to the Spirit-filled disciples, speaking with tongues at Pentecost; to a lame man, healed in the Temple itself; to the Council, where Stephen stands accused; to the city of Samaria, where Philip does signs and wonders; to the synagogues of various cities, where Paul preaches; to the gates of Lystra, where Christian missionaries are thought to be Greek gods descended to earth; to the local magistrates, where Paul and his companions are accused of turning the world upside down; to the Areopagus, where it is reported a new teaching has reached Athens; to the theater of Ephesus, where the mob shouts for two hours, "Great is Artemis of the Ephesians!"; to the Temple once more, where the crowd wave their garments, throw dust in the air, and cry: "Away with such a fellow from the earth!" Here are stonings, escapes from prison, shipwreck, riot, the drama of the courtroom, the pomp of rulers, the plight of the poor. Here are sermons and defenses, prayers and letters, crucial debates and deliberative decisions—all of tremendous theological importance. And the whole drama is played on a stage as wide as Caesar's empire.

The Message of Acts

The Church as Chosen People

Throughout the Bible God reveals himself in connection with a people he has chosen. It may offend us to think that the universal God who made all men acts in a special way toward one particular people. But this theme runs from one end of the Bible to the other, and if we try to remove it we have no Bible left.

As the drama of the Bible unfolds, we see a succession of chosen peoples. They are chosen, not to be God's pets, but to be his servants, that he may bless all men through them. First there is the nation Israel. When the nation breaks Covenant, it is cast off in captivity, but a chosen Remnant returns. When the Remnant fails to perform its mission, God calls out of it his Son, his Chosen One. Jesus then gathers about him a new Remnant, the little flock of disciples. Thus far, God's Chosen People have all been of the Jewish community. But now, out of the preaching of the disciples, a new People of God comes into existence: the Christian Church. And in the Church, the bonds of Jewish nationality are ruptured. Gentiles belong to the People of God. God's Chosen People are no longer identified by their descent from Abraham according to the flesh. But the promises made to Abraham are theirs. The Church, not the Jewish nation, is now the true Israel of God.

What Acts says to Christians of our day, then, is this: You are the People of God. The Scriptures, the Covenant, the promises, belong to you. The call to be God's servant, to suffer redemptively for all mankind, is also laid upon you. Israel's privileges and duties are now yours. The biblical drama did not end far away and long ago; you are playing your part in it here and now.

The Power of the Holy Spirit

Acts also reminds us that the Church has privileges ancient Israel never had. We live after the Resurrection, when the backbone of evil has already been broken and when Jesus already reigns as Lord. As proof of this, he has poured out his Spirit upon the Church. The Church does not carry out her mission in her own power, but in the power of the Spirit. Surely this message is sorely needed by a Church that is more problem-conscious than power-conscious.

To read Acts is to become vitally aware of "the forgotten Person of the Trinity." The title of the book might well read: "The Acts of the Holy Spirit." For he is the main actor. We see the Spirit poured out by the ascended Lord on the Day of Pentecost. And from then on it is the Spirit who directs and corrects, who guides and blocks, who empowers the Church and the individuals who make it up.

The Unity of the Church

Again and again Acts speaks to situations in our own day. "The great new fact of our time" is the Church's struggle to overcome her divisions and find a new unity in Christ. For this struggle Acts has a definite message. Acts clearly shows that the seeds of disunity were in the Church at the very earliest period. Yet unity was maintained. The basis of unity in Acts was not a common doctrinal statement, nor yet common forms of worship and government. It was the common sharing in the Spirit. Wherever the gifts of the Spirit appeared, the early Christians felt compelled to acknowledge the presence of the Church—the one Church of which all were members.

God Shows No Partiality

Certainly one of the great issues of our day is racism. Acts speaks to that. It relates the efforts of Jewish Christians to cling to a faith that would exclude those of other races. And it shows the Spirit leading them against their wills to new insights and new feelings. One by one the barriers topple: "God has shown me that I should not call any man common or unclean" . . . "Truly I perceive that God shows no partiality" . . . "Who was I that I could withstand God?" . . . "He [God] made no distinction between us and them" . . . "[God] made from one every nation of men" (10:28; 10:34; 11:17; 15:9; 17:26).

Instances could be multiplied of the very direct way in which Acts speaks to us where we live. It is more than a history of Christian beginnings. It is more than an answer to an acute theological problem of the first century. It is the Word of God to his Church here and now. To study it is to become involved in the ongoing drama of God's purpose.

OUTLINE

COMMENTARY

THE PRELUDE TO THE WITNESS

Acts 1:1-26

Jesus' Final Promise and Command (1:1-14)

The Transition to Book Two (1:1-2)

Acts begins with a transition rather than a preface. We have explained in the Introduction that Luke is Book One and Acts is Book Two of a single work. Acts is not an afterthought. It is not a sequel, published after the first book had turned out well and its readers demanded more. It is the second volume of a work that was planned to go together and to present a single message to its readers. We are not surprised, then, that Acts has no separate preface of its own. What Luke needed to do at this point was to assure his readers that they had picked up the right papyrus roll, that this second roll properly followed the one they had just finished.

So Luke begins with a mention of his "first book." He says it dealt with the deeds and teachings of Jesus up to the Ascension. This is a very brief but good summary of Luke's Gospel. We are struck with the unusual phrase: "all that Jesus *began* to do and teach." It is easy to overemphasize this. The Greek Old Testament, with which Luke was quite familiar, often uses "began to" without any special meaning. But certainly the whole Book of Acts shows that Luke did not regard the Ascension as the *end* of Jesus' deeds and teachings. Through the Spirit, Jesus continues to live and work in his Church.

The first book was addressed to "most excellent Theophilus" (Luke 1:3). By repeating this address at the beginning of Book Two, Luke further assures his readers that they are on the right track. Who was Theophilus? Theophilus means "lover of God" or "loved by God," and therefore some have thought that Luke-Acts is dedicated to all Christians. However, Theophilus was a real name, widely used in Luke's day among Greeks and Greek-speaking Jews. Moreover, ancient writers usually dedicated their books to definite individuals, even though they were writing for the general public. This means that Theophilus was probably a real person. By "most excellent," Luke shows he was a man of

high rank. (Compare "his Excellency the governor Felix" in
Acts 23:26 and "most excellent Festus" in Acts 26:25.) From
Luke 1:4 we learn that Theophilus had received some instruction in the Christian faith. Throughout the Gospel and Acts,
Luke assumes that Theophilus and his other readers are thoroughly familiar with the Old Testament. Possibly, then, Theophilus had for some years been a "God-fearer," a Gentile who attended the Jewish synagogue and studied the Jewish Scriptures.
We would like to know more about him, but these are all the
facts we have.

Luke finishes orienting his readers by retelling at the beginning of his second book several of the incidents with which he
closed Book One. These include the Resurrection appearances,
the parting commission, the Ascension, and the return of the disciples to Jerusalem. Thus the transition really continues through
verse 14.

The Resurrection Appearances (1:3-5)

These verses seem at first a very bald summary. Yet verse 3
contains two important items that are found nowhere else. One is
the definite period of forty days (compare the forty days of
temptation in Luke 4:2). The other is the idea that Jesus appeared to his disciples often enough to have a real teaching
ministry to them after the Resurrection.

The theme of Jesus' teaching during the forty days is the old
theme of his earthly ministry: the Kingdom of God. Luke gives
us few details of what he taught. The most reliable clue can be
found in Luke 24:25-27, 44-47: Jesus interpreted to them in all
the Scriptures the things concerning himself. When the disciples
emerged into public life again, the center of their message was
no longer, as in Jesus' lifetime, the Kingdom of God which was
drawing near. It was the King himself: God's Servant who suffered and had been exalted to God's right hand. And with an
amazing grasp of the Old Testament, they were able to show that
all that had happened did so according to the Scriptures. This
marked change of message and growth of understanding is most
easily explained by tracing it to the creative mind of Jesus himself.

Verses 4 and 5 re-emphasize two things: the command not to
leave Jerusalem and the promise of baptism with the Holy Spirit
(compare Luke 24:49). It was very natural that the disciples

would want to leave Jerusalem. It was not their home. The men who had killed Jesus were in power there, and his followers could expect opposition and persecution. We should expect Jesus' followers to return to Galilee. According to some records, they did (Matt. 28; John 21). But the return to Galilee was only temporary. For it is a historical fact that the Church arose, not in Galilee, but in Jerusalem. The best explanation is the one given here: the disciples felt themselves under the Lord's orders to stay there.

They were to wait in Jerusalem for the baptism of the Holy Spirit. What Jesus promises here had been promised by John the Baptist (Luke 3:16). Even before that, it was "the promise of the Father" in such Scriptures as Isaiah 44:2-5; Ezekiel 39: 28-29; and Joel 2:28-29. It means an outpouring of the Spirit on all of God's people, endowing them with power from on high.

We leave these three verses unsatisfied. How much more we would like to know! How hazy still is our idea of just what the Risen Christ was like! How many puzzles are unsolved! Like all the records of Jesus' post-Resurrection appearances, this one is fragmentary.

But the heart of the matter is beyond doubt: "To them he presented himself alive after his passion [suffering and death] by many proofs" (1:3). These experiences, however mysterious, were not the products of the disciples' fevered imagination. These men were not self-deluded. All the evidence points to the fact that they had never imagined such a thing would happen. They were extremely reluctant to believe one another or their own senses when it did happen. The great fact of the Resurrection, which we find them proclaiming throughout the rest of Acts, was not their invention. They had been driven to believe it against all logic and common sense and all the experience of the human race. Only the real appearance of the Risen Lord can account for their faith.

The Parting Commission (1:6-8)

Just before Jesus leaves his disciples for the last time, a remarkable conversation takes place. "Lord," they ask him, "will you at this time restore the kingdom to Israel?" (1:6). In the light of the centuries that have followed, we can pity them for their blindness and slowness to learn. But it was a very natural question for them to ask. They rightly understood Jesus' resurrection as God's decisive victory over all the forces of evil. Would it not be immediately followed by the complete and visible establishment of his Kingdom? The prophets and even Jesus himself had said things which would lead them to regard the Resurrection as the opening act of the final drama. In the same way, it was natural for them to think of Israel as the center of God's coming Kingdom. It is so pictured in the Old Testament, and Jesus' own ministry had been largely confined to Israel.

Jesus' answer is a gentle correction of both of these misunderstandings. First, to their overeagerness for the End, he replies simply that they cannot know the length of time nor the key moments which the Father has fixed by his own authority (1:7). Is there not a word of caution here for the attempt to read the Bible as a timetable? Second, to their overly patriotic zeal for Israel, he responds by challenging them with a witness which is to begin in Israel but which will extend to the end of the earth (1:8; compare Luke 24:47). No longer will Israel wait for the nations to come to her, bringing gifts to Jerusalem (see Isa. 2:3; 45:14; 60:4-7); instead, the witnesses of Jesus will go out from Jerusalem to the nations. This change of direction is of untold significance. Can a church which sits on its corner and is content to minister merely to those who come to it claim to be faithful to this command?

Acts 1:8 gathers up the major themes of the whole book in a remarkable way. How important the power of the Holy Spirit is in this book! How much witnessing the book relates, both in general and in the narrow meaning of that word: witnessing in court before hostile legal authorities. The very structure of the book is here in three phrases: "in Jerusalem" (chs. 1-7), "in all Judea and Samaria" (chs. 8-12), "and to the end of the earth" (chs. 13-28).

Acts 1:8 also contains a lesson for our own day which we dare not miss. The power of the Holy Spirit is given for a definite task: the mission of the Church. God does not give the Spirit for the selfish glory or ease of a church or an individual. The power of the Spirit is no magic which we may control for our own purposes. It is a power which controls us. In answer to our prayers for a new outpouring of the Spirit's power, God may well respond: "What do you intend to do with it?"

The Ascension (1:9-11)

The time came when the Resurrection appearances of Jesus ceased. "Where is he?" was the most urgent question his followers faced. Were his life and death and resurrection just another incident in history? Had he now vanished from view, making no real change in the order of things? So it might appear, but they were convinced otherwise. He is now, they declared, at the very center of things. He has gone to sit at the right hand of God, in the position of supreme authority in the universe. This triumphant faith in an exalted Jesus is found everywhere in the New Testament (see Acts 2:33; 5:31; 7:55-56; Rom. 8:34; Eph. 1:20; Col. 3:1; Heb. 1:3; 12:2; I Peter 3:22; Rev. 3:21).

Luke is the only writer who puts this faith in the form of a concrete story of the ascension of Jesus. The scene is the Mount of Olives (1:12). Just after the final commission has been given, Jesus is lifted up, and a cloud, the symbol of all that is mysterious and beyond human understanding, takes him out of sight. The disciples remain, gazing into heaven. Two men in white robes appear (compare Luke 24:4, 23). They are God's angelic messengers, bringing the promise that Jesus will some day return in the same way.

There could be no more natural or beautiful way for a first-century Christian to describe Jesus' final parting from his disciples. Yet to some modern minds it has presented many difficulties. We know that the earth is a ball whirling through space. We cannot locate heaven as "up" or earth as "down." This need not destroy for us the realities of the Ascension story. Heaven is not a part of our space-time universe, but a realm which our space-time minds cannot picture. It is the seat of God's authority, from which he rules the entire universe that he has made. Even the New Testament seems to imply that the place to which Jesus ascended is not to be found in the physical universe, for it says he "ascended far above all the heavens" (Eph. 4:10).

The Return to Jerusalem (1:12-14)

Here Luke finishes retelling the closing scenes of his first book (compare Luke 24:52-53). Acts provides some additional details concerning the life of Jesus' disciples in the days between the Resurrection and the Day of Pentecost. They had their headquarters in an upper room, and imagination is quick to suggest that it may have been the same upper room in which Jesus ate the Last Supper with his own. The chosen Twelve, reduced by the death of Judas to eleven, formed the nucleus of the little band. The women who had been Jesus' constant attendants (see Luke 8:1-3) were there. Perhaps also some of the disciples' wives were included. Jesus' mother was with them, the last glimpse the New Testament affords of her. And, most amazingly, the brothers of Jesus have joined the group. We find their names in Mark 6:3. Some people like to think of Jesus as Mary's only son and explain these brothers as cousins or as sons of Joseph by a former marriage. The most natural meaning is that they were younger sons of Joseph and Mary. However that may be, the Gospels always picture them as failing to understand Jesus and as hostile toward his mission. Now, at the risk of safety and reputation, they have cast in their lot with his despised followers. Unconvinced by his life, they had been conquered by his death and resurrection.

The chief occupation of this waiting group was prayer. It is probable that they attended the set hours of prayer in the Temple (see Luke 24:53 and Acts 2:46), for they had been trained to pray in this way. But there was a new content in their praying. Jesus had spoken of the promise of the Father; and for the fulfillment of that promise, for the baptism with the Holy Spirit, they prayed continually. Until the promise came, they could only wait.

Filling Out the Twelve (1:15-26)

The Twelve Apostles

During his ministry Jesus was followed by a group of disciples, sometimes large and sometimes small. The word "disciple" simply means "learner," and anyone who wished to follow Jesus and listen to his teaching could be a disciple. Out of this large, indefinite number of disciples, Jesus chose a definite group of twelve men. As the oldest record gives it, these twelve were "to be with him, and to be sent out to preach and have authority to cast out demons" (Mark 3:14-15).

Soon these men came to be called apostles. The word "apostle" means one who has been sent out on a special mission. It is easy to see how they got this name, since Jesus had sent them out on a mission during his ministry, and after his death they were given the responsibility for carrying the mission to the ends of the earth. We should note that the word "apostle" is not always restricted to them. The New Testament applies it to other early missionaries, such as Barnabas and Epaphroditus. And it is well known that Paul specifically claimed the title for himself. Nevertheless, when "the apostles" are mentioned, it is usually these twelve men who are meant.

It was not by accident or whim that there were exactly twelve of them. In the Gospels, the most frequent name for them is not "the apostles" but simply "the twelve." As there had been twelve tribes in the Israel of the Old Testament, so there must be twelve apostles in the New Israel, the Christian Church. Luke records in his first book the remembered promise of Jesus that in the Kingdom of God the twelve Apostles would sit on thrones, judging the twelve tribes of Israel (see Luke 22:28-30). It was the importance attached to the number twelve that made it necessary for Judas to be replaced.

Peter Suggests Judas' Replacement (1:15-22)

The filling out of the Twelve begins with a speech by Peter. This address was delivered to the whole assembled company of some 120 persons. This indicates that the appointment was the public concern of the whole fellowship, not just a private affair for the Eleven. No doubt there were other faithful disciples of Jesus in Galilee and elsewhere, but in Jerusalem only 120 could be found. Out of the vast multitudes who had hung upon his word and the scores who had been healed, only these few were faithful after his death. Yet from this small "creative minority" there grew, in a single generation, a Church that made its influence felt to the ends of the known world. Christians above all others should never be discouraged by small numbers.

Peter feels very keenly the theological problem raised by the treachery of Judas. "He was numbered among us, and was allotted his share in this ministry" (1:17). How unthinkable that one who had companied with the Apostles, one who had been appointed by Jesus himself, should fall away! Did this mean that his place was eternally vacant? Must another be appointed to occupy his throne in the judgment? No hasty, on-the-spot explanation will do. Peter seeks an answer in the Scriptures: "Brethren, the scripture had to be fulfilled" (1:16).

At first glance, the answer Peter offers does not satisfy us. He brings forward some verses from the Psalms and tries to show by them that Judas' place among the Twelve is indeed vacant and must be filled. This looks suspiciously like an improper use of the Bible. Has Peter made up his mind that a replacement is necessary, and is he "hunting for texts" to support his opinion? Closer study reveals that he is not. Let us remember that in Peter's day the Bible had not been divided into chapters and verses. He could not use numbers, as we do, to refer to a long passage of Scripture. All he could do was to quote a phrase or sentence and hope that his hearers were so familiar with Scripture that the whole Psalm would come to mind. We do something of this kind when we mention the first line of a familiar hymn and expect our hearers to think of the whole hymn. Peter is referring, then, to the whole of Psalms 69 and 109, or at least to major portions of them.

Both these Psalms picture great and undeserved suffering. In both, two characters stand out: The sufferer and the group or individual who has betrayed him. We cannot be sure who was the original sufferer and who the original traitor; but to the devout Jews of Peter's day, the sufferer was Israel and the traitor was Israel's foes.

Peter goes further. Many details of these Psalms were bound to suggest to him details of the suffering of Jesus which were still fresh in his mind: the enmity of Jesus' own brothers (see Ps. 69:8 and John 7:5); Jesus' zeal for his Father's house (see Ps. 69:9 and Mark 11:15-18); the desertion of all Jesus' friends (see Ps. 69:20 and Mark 14:50); the vinegar given Jesus to drink (see Ps. 69:21 and Mark 15:36); Jesus' prayer for his enemies (see Ps. 109:4 and Luke 23:34); the way Jesus' accusers wagged their heads at him (see Ps. 109:25 and Mark 15:29). But beyond and beneath these detailed correspondences, Peter seems to be sensing a great principle which becomes increasingly clear in the sermons he preaches: Jesus is himself the true Israel. Jesus is what Israel was called to be, but never fully became: the Servant of the Lord. Therefore, all that is said of Israel's suffering in the Old Testament can rightfully be applied to Jesus. And the curses which are pronounced on those who have wrongfully betrayed Israel apply to Judas, who betrayed Jesus. This, or something like it, is the reasoning behind Peter's use of Scripture.

The record of Judas' death in verses 18-19 is clearly an explanation by Luke for Theophilus, not a part of Peter's remarks, and so rightly belongs in parentheses. It gives a very different account of Judas' death from the one found in Matthew 27:3-10. It is possible to harmonize the two stories by saying that Judas first hanged himself and then burst open when he was cut down. But it is perhaps simpler to recognize that two stories circulated in the Early Church and we have no means of determining which is more accurate. The essential facts are that he met a violent end and that the "Field of Blood" was purchased with the reward money.

Peter concludes by laying down the qualifications for Judas' replacement: the person to be selected must have accompanied the Apostles during the entire ministry of Jesus from the baptism of John to the Ascension. Such a man would be adequately equipped to perform the most essential function of an Apostle: to be a witness of the Resurrection.

The Selection of Matthias (1:23-26)

Our attention is caught here by the use of the lot. It was natural for men raised in the Old Testament faith to use lots. The land had been divided and kings had been chosen by lot. The usual method was to write the names on stones which were shaken out of a jar.

Let us be clear that the choice was not totally by lot. It was not a matter of letting the lot fall on any one of the 120. Certain qualifications were laid down by Peter. The group then put forward two men whom they felt fulfilled the qualifications. Earnest prayer was made that the Lord would indicate his will through the lot. Only then and under these restrictions was the lot cast.

Why was this practice so quickly abandoned? We have no further record in the New Testament of the choosing of leaders by lot. Perhaps this was because the Twelve were unique. They had been chosen, not by the congregation, but by Jesus during his ministry. Only in filling out the Twelve was it necessary to secure an appointment directly from the ascended Lord, not mediated through any human being. Or perhaps after the Spirit was given, his guidance made lots unnecessary.

The important point is that in abandoning the lot, the Church did not abandon the idea that its leaders must be chosen by Christ. Whether these leaders are marked out by vote, appoint-

ment, or some gift of the Spirit, they are ultimately chosen by
the Lord of the Church. We need to reclaim in our day this awesome sense that the final appointment of Church officers is made
by Christ himself.

THE WITNESS IN JERUSALEM

Acts 2:1—8:3

The Day of Pentecost (2:1-42)

The Feast

An important part of the Jewish religion was the observance
of feasts and special days. The three major feasts of the year
were the Feast of the Passover, the Feast of Weeks, and the Feast
of Tabernacles. Pentecost (the fiftieth day) is another name for
the Feast of Weeks, which was a harvest festival held just seven
weeks (49 days) after the Passover.

Following the Passover Feast at which Jesus had been killed,
the population of Jerusalem had shrunk to its normal figure of
about 50,000. But now crowds thronged through the gates again.
Every inch of lodging space was filled. As pilgrims from all over
the world pressed into the city, the temporary population may
have risen as high as a million. The Passover crowd had been
mainly Palestinian Jews. But by Pentecost the weather permitted
sea travel, and Jews from all the lands about the Mediterranean
converged on Jerusalem.

The Outpouring of the Spirit (2:1-4)

Unnoticed amid the bustling mass of pilgrims, the little band
of Jesus' followers continued to wait for the baptism of the Holy
Spirit. Suddenly, when they were all together in some place
we cannot identify, the Spirit came. This is undoubtedly the most
important event in Acts and the most difficult to describe.

Those who live through a crisis in God's dealings with men,
like the Exodus, or the Resurrection, or Pentecost, can never
fully describe it. They see things and hear things and feel things
in their hearts for which there are no words. Yet they must report these experiences in concrete terms, since we really do not
understand any other terms.

So we find the coming of the Spirit compared to the sound of a mighty wind and to the sight of tongues of flame. Who can offer a better description? The Spirit is like the wind: uncontrollable, mysterious, powerful, seen only in his effects. In Hebrew and in Greek the same word means both "wind" and "spirit." The Spirit is also like the flame: cleansing and consuming, awesome and dangerous.

Notice the repeated emphasis on the fact that the Spirit was given to the whole group. "They were all together in one place" . . . "it filled all the house" . . . "resting on each one of them" . . . and "they were all filled with the Holy Spirit." There was no question here of a few first-class believers elevated above the mass of second-class believers by individual possession of the Spirit. The Spirit was poured out on the whole fellowship and thus was distributed to the individuals who made up the fellowship.

This observation helps us answer the most puzzling question about Pentecost. How could the Spirit "come" at Pentecost when he had always been in the world? Did not Luke in his first book show Jesus performing his ministry in the power of the Spirit? (Luke 4:14). Was not Jesus, indeed, conceived by the Holy Spirit? (Luke 1:35). Are there not many stories in the Old Testament of how the Spirit fell upon the leaders and prophets of Israel? Was not the Spirit at work in the creation itself? (Gen. 1:2). What is the new thing, then, that happened at Pentecost?

Let us be clear that Luke is not saying that the Spirit first came into existence on the Day of Pentecost. His point is that the Spirit was given then in a way in which he had never been given before. No one was more aware than the people of Israel themselves that the Spirit had not been given to them in any complete or final sense. Never in the Old Testament was the Spirit poured out on all the people; only to the chosen leaders was the Spirit given. And the gift was temporary. When the immediate crisis passed, the Spirit departed.

These fleeting experiences of the Spirit only increased the longing of the Old Testament saints for the day when the Spirit would be completely and permanently bestowed. Thus Moses cries out: "Would that all the LORD's people were prophets, that the LORD would put his spirit upon them!" (Num. 11:29). The Messiah, they hoped, would be different from all others because the Spirit would *rest* upon him (Isa. 11:1-3). And Joel looked for the day when the Spirit would be poured out, not just on a few leaders, but on all flesh, even the menservants and maid-servants (Joel 2:28-29).

On the Day of Pentecost, the longing of the Old Testament was fulfilled. The Spirit came, not to some individual in crisis, but to an assembled people. "They were all filled with the Holy Spirit." The Spirit came, not temporarily, but to dwell in their midst, to be the bond of their fellowship, the secret source of their common life, the power for their mission to the world, the witness to their preaching. We can see now how it could truly be said that before this "the Spirit had not been given" (John 7:39).

The Gift of Tongues (2:5-13)

Only those who received the Spirit seem to have heard the wind or seen the flames, but one effect of his coming was im-mediately evident to outsiders: the gift of tongues.

There are many accounts of this in the New Testament. Time and again believers were so overwhelmed with the mighty works of God that ordinary words could not express what they felt. They burst out into ecstatic speech; rapid phrases, sounds, even groans, were all run together. Most people could not under-stand them. But they were trying to speak to God, and they were sure that he could understand what they wanted to say. This often occurred when people heard the gospel for the first time, but it could take place whenever the believers gathered for worship. No one could speak this way just by trying to; it was clearly the work of something other than a man's normal faculties. It was regarded as a gift of the Spirit. The clearest description of the gift of tongues is found in I Corinthians 14. It has recurred in the Church down to the present day, especially in times of genuine revival.

Now, in one way, the account of what happened at Pentecost sounds like the typical gift of tongues. They all spoke "in other tongues, as the Spirit gave them utterance" (vs. 4). Some who heard them said they were filled with new wine (vs. 13). Peter begins his speech by explaining that they are not drunk. This agrees with Paul's description: "If . . . all speak in tongues, and outsiders or unbelievers enter, will they not say that you are mad?" (I Cor. 14:23).

But there is a difference here. Here, and here only, the gift of tongues is described as a gift of foreign languages. Men from every nation under heaven hear the simple Galilean disciples speaking a great variety of different dialects. The puzzle deepens when we realize that such a miracle was unnecessary. In a few moments Peter addresses the crowd in Aramaic, the common language of the Near East in that time, and everyone understands him perfectly! Nor is there any record that the Apostles in all their subsequent missionary work ever used this miraculous gift; simple Aramaic and Greek were sufficient.

What are we to make of this? All sorts of answers have been suggested. We may reject the suggestion that Luke was not familiar with the usual gift of tongues, for he describes it without any suggestion of foreign languages in Acts 10:44-48 and 19:6. Perhaps the crowd on this occasion was given the gift of interpreting tongues; perhaps they were in such close sympathy with the speakers that the essential message got over to them, even in unintelligible sounds. Or perhaps here Luke has let his theology run away with his history. He sees clearly the inner meaning of the gift of the Spirit. It is the dawn of a new age when men of all nations will be brought into the People of God. The ancient breach made among men at the Tower of Babel, when God confused their language (Gen. 11:1-9), is potentially healed by the gift of the Spirit. So Luke may be recording what must inevitably happen as a result of Pentecost as though it had happened on the day itself.

However that may be, the ultimate effect of Pentecost has certainly been a miracle of languages. The Christian missionary movement has reduced many a language to writing for the first time, has made the illiterate masses literate, has translated the Bible into over a thousand dialects—all so men can say: "We hear them telling in our own tongues the mighty works of God."

The Speeches in Acts

Following the gift of tongues, Peter preaches a long sermon. Before analyzing it in detail, it will be helpful to notice the speeches in Acts in general. Someone has counted up 24 speeches in the book, amounting to roughly one-fifth of the whole volume. They provide variety to the narrative and contain probably the best-known and best-loved verses in Acts.

When we think about it, we realize that in the ancient world no one ever tried to record a lengthy speech word for word. There were no tape recorders, no court stenographers. Listeners simply formed an impression of the important points the speaker made, remembered them, and summarized in their own words. Luke was not even present when most of the speeches he records were made. He had to rely on someone's recollection of what was said.

Under these circumstances most ancient historians frankly made up speeches and put them in the mouths of their heroes. Luke has been accused of doing this, and it is certain that the speeches are very much in the same literary style as the rest of the book.

However, there are reasons for believing that Luke was much more careful than other historians of his day to present faithfully the main points of what was actually said. Much of his Gospel is based on Mark. We can see that he improves Mark's Greek and puts many things into his own style. But he rarely changes the essential meaning. And he is particularly careful to give the sayings of Jesus accurately. It is at least probable that he was just as careful with the speeches in Acts, whether he had written notes or only oral accounts to go by.

In the sermon that we are about to read, and in the other sermons of the Apostles, we have further evidence of Luke's substantial accuracy. From Paul's letters we can reconstruct the theology of those who were Apostles before him. Paul argues from what they preached, and he builds his own more complicated system on it. The theology of the sermons of Peter in Acts is basically the same as the primitive theology to which Paul appeals. Luke, writing from thirty to sixty years after Pentecost, could hardly have made up, out of his head, speeches which would reflect so accurately that early theology.

We may be confident, then, that the sermons in Acts are accurate summaries, in Luke's style, of the preaching of the Early Church. As such, their value to us can hardly be overestimated. For this early preaching (called in many recent books by its Greek name, *kerygma*) is the basis from which the whole New Testament developed. It represents, as nothing else can, the essential core of the Christian faith.

"This Is What Was Spoken by the Prophet" (2:14-21)

We turn now to the details of Peter's sermon. The Eleven stand with him, a symbol that he speaks for them all. It is significant that in Greek the word "addressed" in verse 14 is the same as "utterance" in verse 4. Peter's sermon, no less than the tongues, is the Spirit's work. The more we study it and notice its striking results, the surer we are that it is the greater of the two wonders.

Peter begins with what had drawn the crowd: the gift of tongues. This strange behavior, he says, can be explained. It is not drunkenness; it is the fulfillment of prophecy. He then quotes Joel 2:28-32. The first part of this passage is completely appropriate. It expresses clearly the Old Testament longing for a time when God will pour out his Spirit, not on a few exceptional individuals, but on his whole people. This, says Peter, is exactly what has happened.

But what are we to make of the rest of the quotation, verses 19-21? These cosmic disturbances did not occur at Pentecost. Why did Peter bother to quote them? These were well-known descriptions of the final End, as readers familiar with Revelation will recognize. Joel is saying that the outpouring of the Spirit will be a sign that the last days have begun. And that is just what Peter believes, for at the beginning of his quotation he has even substituted the words "in the last days" for "afterward" (or "after these things") which stood in Joel.

The sense of living in the last days marks the whole New Testament. After so many centuries have passed we are apt to conclude that the early Christians were mistaken. Certainly the End did not come as soon as they expected. Yet there is a precious truth here we must not lose. Christians ought not to live as though the death and resurrection of Christ have made no real difference. That Event ushered in a new kind of time—the last days—for us to live in. That the last days have lasted so long does not change their essential nature. These are the days when the powers of the End are already at work. These are the days when the Kingdom of God, for which men hoped so long, already exists. These are the days when Christ, having won his victory, already rules. These are the days when whoever calls on the name of the Lord shall be saved—Jew or Gentile. The morning newspaper and the routine of our daily work seem to deny this. The kingdoms of this world are still very real, and we must play our part in them. But the Christian knows that the backbone of their power was broken long ago and that the real authority belongs to Christ. The greatest evidence for this is the presence of the Spirit in the Church.

God's Act in Jesus (2:22-24)

After quoting Joel, Peter reviews briefly the facts of Jesus' life: his public ministry with its mighty works, his crucifixion by men outside the Law (the Romans), and his resurrection. Peter's emphasis is on God's action in all this. God did the signs and wonders through Jesus. God planned the Crucifixion. God raised him up. It is hard for us to appreciate the marvel of this way of looking at such tragic events. How could the Early Church so quickly look at the cruel, unjust, judicial murder of Jesus and see in it the plan and foreknowledge of God? Luke's suggestion is that only the Risen Christ himself could have made them look at it in this way (Luke 24:25-27).

Jesus Is the Christ (2:25-32)

Peter now turns to Psalm 16. We have already noticed, in discussing Acts 1:20, that reference is usually to a whole Psalm, not just the phrases quoted.

When we study this Psalm we are struck once more with the aptness of Peter's selection. In the Old Testament there was little hope of life after death. The standard belief was that the dead maintained a shadowy existence in Sheol. Sheol is not to be confused with the later idea of hell, that is, a place of fire and torment. It was merely the grave-land, the place of weakness and shadows and meaninglessness. Men were thought to be cut off from God there (see Ps. 88). "Hades" in Acts 2:27 is simply the Greek word for Sheol.

Now in Psalm 16 there is a break-through. The psalmist rises above the common belief in Sheol to a genuine hope for life beyond death. He has enjoyed such an intimate companionship with God in this life that he refuses to believe death can break it. In daring faith he cries that God will not abandon him to Sheol (Ps. 16:10).

Peter urges that David, who according to popular tradition wrote the Psalms, did not completely fulfill what he wrote. He died and his tomb was known. He must, then, have spoken of someone else. Who would that be, if not the Christ, who was to be one of his descendants? (see Ps. 132:11). The resurrection of Jesus, of which the Apostles are witnesses, has made actual and real what David hoped for. This proves Jesus to be indeed *the Christ*.

"The Christ" is a title; it had here not yet become a part of Jesus' name. It is simply the Greek form of the Hebrew title "the Messiah." The Gospels picture for us the feverish way in which the people of Jesus' day were looking for the Messiah, the promised Deliverer whom God would send. Even during Jesus' lifetime, the disciples had recognized that he must be the Messiah. Peter had declared at Caesarea Philippi: "You are the Christ" (Mark 8:29). But Jesus had avoided the title and forbidden them to use it, much preferring the mysterious phrase, "Son of man." Now, however, after the Resurrection, the ban on using the title is over. The early preachers come forward immediately to prove from a variety of Old Testament Scriptures that Jesus was and is the promised Messiah.

The proof advanced here, where the tomb of David is the key, rests on the empty tomb of Jesus. The whole Christian movement could have been stopped by its enemies finally and completely by one simple thing: all they had to do was to produce the body of Jesus. They could not. All arguments that the Resurrection was only wishful thinking on the part of Jesus' followers fall right here.

Jesus Is Lord (2:33-36)

In quoting Psalm 16, Peter stopped just short of the final line, but it was surely familiar to him and to his hearers: "In thy right hand are pleasures for evermore." Jesus, being raised from the dead, is at the right hand of God. As we have seen, this is the essential truth behind the story of the Ascension. Jesus occupies the position of supreme authority in the universe, right next to the throne of God himself!

In this position of authority, he has received from the Father the promise of the Holy Spirit. What God had formerly bestowed partially and temporarily, is now handed over to Jesus to bestow fully and permanently. And it is Jesus who, in the strange events of Pentecost, is pouring out the Spirit on his Church. This is most important for the whole New Testament doctrine of the Holy Spirit. From this point on, he is the *Spirit of Jesus.* He takes Jesus' place in the company of his followers. His character is the character of Jesus. His teaching is the teaching of Jesus. His acts are the acts of Jesus. What Jesus began to do and teach in the days of his flesh, Jesus continues to do and teach through the Spirit in the Church.

Peter now turns to the Psalms once again. Pursuing the theme that Jesus is at God's right hand, he refers to Psalm 110. This Psalm is quoted more in the New Testament than any other. Peter uses the same logic as before: David speaks of a "Lord" who sits at the Lord's right hand; David did not ascend into heaven; he could not, then, mean himself; he must mean Jesus; therefore Jesus is properly to be called *Lord*.

This title had an even wider meaning than "the Christ." The Jews used it, even as we do in our familiar English translations, in place of the sacred name of God: Yahweh. To use this title for Jesus was to place him in the closest kind of relation with God himself. There was also a practical force to this title which the early Christians felt just as keenly as they did the theological force. Caesar called himself "Lord." As "Lord," he exercised authority and commanded obedience from all the civilized world. By the end of the first century, he was to command worship of himself as "Lord." To call Jesus Lord, therefore, was to assert that ultimate authority and obedience and worship belong to Jesus, not to Caesar. As the Church spread through the Roman Empire, its earliest confession of faith was: "Jesus is Lord" (see Rom. 10:9). And when the persecutions began, it was because of this confession that the martyrs went to the stake and into the arena. They would not worship Caesar as Lord; that title belonged to Jesus alone.

Both Psalms and both arguments are brought to a head in Peter's masterful conclusion: "God has made him both Lord and Christ." This is the primitive way of thinking about Jesus. His existence with the Father before his birth, his nature as both human and divine at the same time—these and other problems had to be thought out later. The early preachers had known the man Jesus. The Resurrection and the events of Pentecost satisfied them that God had made him both Lord and Christ. That was enough to go on.

"What Shall We Do?" (2:37-40)

Peter's sermon is not exactly the kind of sermon we are used to today. Its illustrations and arguments may seem to us strange and unappealing. But to the men who heard him, steeped in the Old Testament, eagerly looking for the Messiah, vaguely uneasy about the part some of them had played in Jesus' death, it was a thunderclap. They were cut to the heart. Suddenly they saw themselves guilty of the world's most enormous crime. They had crucified the Messiah. The End and the judgment of God stared them in the face. "Brethren," they cried to Peter and the rest of the Apostles, "what shall we do?"

This gave Peter the chance to apply his sermon. He issued three ringing imperatives. The first is: "Repent." This does not mean, "Be sorry for what you've done." It means, "Change your mind. Get a new sense of values. Reverse your direction."

The second imperative is: "Be baptized every one of you in the name of Jesus Christ." This was something new. Jesus himself had been baptized by John, but had not made baptism a condition of discipleship. Yet from the Day of Pentecost on, it becomes the standard rite by which men enter the Christian fellowship. It is not easy to say just how this came about.

The recent discovery of the Dead Sea Scrolls sheds some light here. They were written by a group of earnest Jews who felt that the bulk of the Jewish nation was hopelessly corrupt. They withdrew into the wilderness and devoted themselves to a study of the Law. The laws of ceremonial cleansing were of great interest to them. When someone wanted to join their community, he underwent repeated ceremonies of washing. This was to cleanse him of the corruption into which Israel had fallen and to admit him to the community of purified men.

John the Baptist, like the men who wrote the Dead Sea Scrolls, felt that the nation Israel had departed from God. They were a "brood of vipers" (Luke 3:7). He, too, demanded a ceremonial cleansing of his hearers. They must wash off Israel's corruption. But they were baptized, not into membership in an existing community, but for deliverance from the wrath to come. They were baptized in preparation for the coming of the Messiah. Baptism marked them out for a future community. It made them eligible for a later baptism with the Holy Spirit when the Messiah came. Thus John's baptism was a preparatory rite.

After the descent of the Spirit at Pentecost had marked out the Messiah's people, the Apostles reinstituted baptism. But this time it was not a preparatory rite. It was an actual initiating into the people of the Messiah. "The name of Jesus Christ" was called upon them and they became his.

Two effects are tied to baptism here. One is the forgiveness of sins, which had also been emphasized in John's baptism. The other is the reception of the Holy Spirit, for which John's baptism had been only a preparation. Here it seems that from Pentecost on, the baptism of the Holy Spirit normally accompanies or immediately follows the outward ceremony of baptism with water. There are exceptions to this, as we shall see (Acts 8:16; 10:47; and 19:1-7).

Peter is at pains to explain that the promise of the Holy Spirit is not just to those on whom he first fell, but to new converts and to their children. Nor was it essential to have been in Jerusalem on Pentecost to receive the Spirit. Those far distant could still receive him when they were baptized. In fact, "every one whom the Lord our God calls to him" would receive the Spirit. The Spirit has been given to the Messiah's people. And when, by baptism, a believer enters the number of the Messiah's people, he enters into their common possession of the Spirit.

The third imperative bears this out still further: "Save yourselves from this crooked generation." Peter is quoting Deuteronomy 32:5:

"They have dealt corruptly with him,
    they are no longer his children because of their blemish;
    they are a perverse and crooked generation."

He is saying that the Jewish nation as a whole has forfeited its position as God's People. To repent and to receive baptism in the name of Jesus Christ is to be separated from an Israel that is hopelessly corrupt, and to be initiated into the true Israel which the coming of the Spirit has now clearly marked off.

The Apostolic Preaching

We are now at the end of Peter's sermon. We have analyzed this example of the early preaching in great detail, because it is typical of all the sermons that follow.

This sermon is not a series of propositions or general truths, such as that God is good, man is sinful, murder is wrong. It is a piece of news! God has entered decisively into human life; God has acted in a new and startling way; God has done something he never did before! Small wonder that this message was called "the gospel," which means "the good news." The early preachers were like a man who stops his neighbor on the street, shakes him by the shoulders, and cries: "Something wonderful has happened!" We may summarize the "news" as follows: The promises of God to the prophets and psalmists are being fulfilled right

now! The last days have begun! It was God who worked in the
ministry of Jesus, who planned his death, who raised him from
the dead. We can witness to that! God has exalted Jesus to his
right hand and made him Lord and Christ. The Messiah's people are now being marked out from a corrupt Israel by the outpouring of the Spirit.

The proclamation of this news always calls for decision: Repent! Be baptized! Leave your corrupt society and enter the
Messiah's community! The news is not told for sentiment or en-
tertainment or to satisfy curiosity. It drives men into a corner
where they must either believe and obey this Lord or reject him.
After what has happened, life cannot go on just as it was.

Should this not be the essence of the Church's message today?
We may find new forms and new illustrations, but our task as we
face the world in this century is the same—to declare that God
has done something unique in Christ and that men cannot ignore it; they must take sides.

The Great Ingathering (2:41-42)

Now came the greatest demonstration of the Spirit's power.
Peter's invitation was immediately accepted by some three thousand people. The seeds of this harvest were not all sown on the
Day of Pentecost. Many of these men had probably heard Jesus
speak, some may have been healed by him, others watched him
die. As soon as an authentic body of his followers was marked
out, they were eager to join it.

Immediately they were caught up in a new quality of life.
With that singlehearted enthusiasm which only the Spirit gives,
they devoted themselves "to the apostles' teaching and fellowship, to the breaking of bread and the prayers" (2:42).

The Apostles' teaching (called in many recent books by
its Greek name: *didache*) was distinct from their preaching
(*kerygma*). It was addressed to believers, as the preaching was
addressed to those outside. But its subject was the same: the
wonderful act of God in Jesus. The meaning of this act for the
faith of believers was explored. And the suitable ethical response
men should make in their daily lives was pointed out. Sayings of
Jesus himself were remembered and applied to the new situation
which Pentecost had brought about. The New Testament itself,
which is mainly written for believers, is a later and expanded example of what the teaching was like.

"The fellowship" was not a matter of patting one another on the back and singing, "Your friends are my friends." It was a deep sharing of common life. Their participation in the one Spirit lay at the root of this. Paul describes it by saying: "By one Spirit we were all baptized into one body . . . and all were made to drink of one Spirit" (I Cor. 12:13). What they had in common became more important than anything which might divide them.

"The breaking of bread" and "the prayers" are phrases describing the worship of the Early Church. These points will be discussed more fully under 2:43-47.

The Birthday of the Church

The word "church" first occurs in Acts 5:11; but by then it is evident that the Church has been in existence for some time. Just when did the Church begin? Many different answers have been given, but the usual one is that Pentecost is "the birthday of the Church." Can this be so? Were not the disciples of Jesus during his lifetime in some sense the Church? Cannot the Church be traced all the way back to Abraham?

Much depends on how we use our terms. On the one hand, the Church is linked to the People of God of all ages. As stated in the Introduction, all through the Bible God is seeking for a people of his own who will be his servants for the redemption of the world. Israel, the Remnant, Jesus, the disciples, and the Church are successively the People of God. We may poetically speak, as Luther and Calvin loved to do, of any link in that chain as "the Church."

But, on the other hand, the Church is different from anything that had gone before. Between the Church and Israel, between the Church and the disciples of the days of Jesus' flesh, has fallen the Event: the death and resurrection of Jesus. The Church is the People of God of "the last days." She is obedient to a Lord who sits at the right hand of God. He has poured out upon her the Spirit, to dwell fully and permanently in her midst. Such a People of God had not existed before. In this sense, Pentecost may justly be taken as "the birthday of the Church."

Opposition from the Authorities (2:43—4:31)

The Common Life of the Believers (2:43-47)

Luke now gives us a general description of life in the Early Church. All the verbs in this paragraph express continuous action: fear kept coming on every soul; wonders and signs kept being done; people kept selling their goods; and so on. This is the way they lived together over a considerable period of time.

First off, the general population stood in awe of the Church. They were afraid to oppose it. This was because of the "wonders and signs." Throughout the New Testament, wonders and signs are results of the Spirit's power (see Rom. 15:19; Heb. 2:4; and many passages in Acts). They are deeds of such an extraordinary nature that they compel attention, even from those who are hostile. The details are not given here, but from other passages we can guess that healing and casting out unclean spirits were the principal signs and wonders. The skepticism of an age of science plus the abuses of certain modern "faith healers" make it difficult for many to believe in the signs and wonders of the Early Church. Yet even the most critical scholars today are inclined to admit that healing formed a large part of Jesus' ministry. There is little doubt that it was continued by the Apostles. Indeed, if we believe credible witnesses, there has always been an outbreak of healings in connection with the great upsurges of spiritual power in the Church's history.

Luke next draws our attention, in verses 44 and 45, to the so-called "communism" of the Early Church. It is important neither to overestimate nor to underestimate what happened. This was not communism in any modern sense. On the other hand, it was not simple charity as practiced by a modern "Community Chest." It was a sharing between Christian brothers, a sharing so intense that nothing was excluded. A detailed discussion of this will be delayed until many things are made more clear in Acts 4:32—5:11.

We would like to know more about the worship of the Early Church than Luke tells us. But from verses 46 and 47 we learn that it had two main features, the same two mentioned in verse 42. In the first place, the Jerusalem church continued to share in the Jewish worship at the Temple, by attending the regular hours of prayer. We all know from our own experience that it is easier to change our beliefs than the forms of worship to which we have been accustomed from childhood. And why should they change? No one thought, at this point, that by becoming Christians they had ceased to be Jews. On the contrary, they felt they had left a corrupt Israel for the true Israel now being gathered out in the last days. A break with their fathers' custom of worship in the Temple could hardly yet occur to them. The budding self-consciousness of the Church took this form: they attended the Temple together in a distinct group.

Yet already the Temple worship was not enough. What they did not share with the rest of Israel had to be expressed. So the second feature of their worship was the breaking of bread. This was carried out, not in the Temple, but in the homes of believers. These common meals were doubtless related to the sharing of goods. They were a practical method of distributing food to those who otherwise would not have had enough to eat. There was also a social side to these meals, as there always is when people eat together. But there is more here. "Breaking of bread" seems to describe a ceremony reminiscent of the act of Jesus at the feeding of the five thousand (Luke 9:16), on the night before his death (Luke 22:19), and in certain of his post-Resurrection appearances (Luke 24:30; John 21:13). We cannot escape the impression that these common meals included sacramental fellowship with Jesus himself. They looked backward to the table fellowship they had had with him in the flesh. They sensed his presence even now in the Spirit in their midst. And they looked forward to the feast in the Kingdom which he had promised (Luke 22:16). At these daily meals the expectation of his return was at a fever pitch. "Maranatha," they prayed: "Our Lord, come!" (see I Cor. 16:22).

This leads directly to the note of joy which marked the Early Church. Joy is one of the most characteristic fruits of the Spirit. The language used here would indicate that the early Christians were not always dignified in expressing the gladness that filled their hearts. Their joy overflowed. It burst out. They praised God.

All of these features of their common life caused a steady growth. They had "favor with all the people"; they attracted attention; they fascinated men; they had drawing power. "The Lord added to their number day by day those who were being saved." The true secret of evangelistic power lies in the quality of the Church's inner life. Techniques and programs may bring people out to the Church or even outwardly into its membership. But they can be really won only as they see a quality of life which can be found nowhere else. If that life were fully manifest in the Church we may wonder whether men would not break their way into such a Church.

The Healing of the Lame Man (3:1-10)

After describing the life of the Early Church in a general way, Luke selects one particular event of those early days and relates it in considerable detail. It admirably illustrates most of the points he has just made.

In accordance with the general custom of participating in the Temple prayers, Peter and John were going up to the Temple. It was about mid-afternoon, the ninth hour after sunrise. They were greeted with a sight which was common in the East then, as it is now: a beggar, lame from his birth, was being carried to his regular place for begging. The Temple, started by Herod the Great and still in the process of building, was a surpassingly beautiful structure, with its porticoes of graceful columns, its open courts paved with giant stones, its gleaming marble, its decorations of gold, its purple curtains rustling in the breeze. The exact location of the gate "called Beautiful" is hard to determine. It may have been one of the outer gates known otherwise as the Shushan Gate. Or it may have been an inner gate which was famous for its covering of Corinthian brass. At any rate, the misery of the beggar, who was probably in rags and covered with flies, was set off against the splendor of his surroundings.

Peter and John had no money. Probably what little they possessed had been put in the common fund. But there was something more important that they could do for the man. The healing power given to the Church by her Risen Lord burst forth: "In the name of Jesus Christ of Nazareth, walk." Peter takes the man by the hand and raises him. He leaps. He walks. He praises God. This was one of the "wonders and signs." Those who witnessed it and recognized the man were amazed.

The Miracle Explained (3:11-16)

Word quickly spread through the Temple, and all the people ran together. They found the man clinging to Peter and John in

Solomon's Portico. This was one of the colonnades which surrounded the Temple on each side. Peter seized the opportunity to preach another sermon, the second recorded in Acts.

As in his first sermon, Peter begins with the immediate circumstances. He is particularly eager to explain that the power which healed the man is not his or John's. Here is one mark of any genuinely Christian faith-healing. The healer makes no claims for himself and seeks no personal profit or glory. He points beyond himself to Jesus.

This miracle, Peter says, is a sign that the God of our fathers has glorified his servant Jesus. The word "servant" or "child" is the same word that is used in the famous passages about the Servant of the Lord in Isaiah (see, for example, Isa. 49:5-6; 52:13). Peter here claims that that mysterious Figure, despised and rejected by men, wounded for our transgressions, silent before his accusers, innocent in his death, and exalted afterward, has found his fulfillment in Jesus.

In all these sermons it is emphasized that Jesus suffered because of a monstrous human crime. This is more fully developed here than in any other sermon. Peter reminds his hearers that Pilate had decided to release Jesus, but they had betrayed and denied him. They had clamored for Barabbas. They had chosen a criminal in place of the Holy and Righteous One—had chosen a murderer, a life-taker, in place of the Author of life. The name "Righteous One" also refers to the Suffering Servant (see Isa. 53: 11). It is reflected in Matthew 27:19; Luke 23:47; Acts 7:52; 22:14; I Peter 3:18; and I John 2:1. The name "Author" is translated "Leader" in Acts 5:31 and "pioneer" in Hebrews 2: 10; 12:2.

But, says Peter, God has raised him from the dead. This fact can be established by witnesses. And now his very name has a healing power. To his name, not to the disciples, goes the credit for this miracle. Names are important. Even today we say things like, "He has a good name in the community," or "I don't want my name associated with that." But we have to use our imagination to sense the importance of names in the Bible. A man's name expresses his character. It stands in a very real way for the man himself. All his authority, all his power, all his essential self, are caught up in his name. It is not surprising, then, that the name of Jesus was an awesome thing to the early Christians. When they in the name of Jesus Christ of Nazareth told a lame man to walk, they believed the power of Jesus himself was present and would act. Verse 16 is a very confusing verse to translate. The important point is that faith is brought into connection with the name. For all its awesome power, the name is not a magic spell. Faith must operate in the situation.

The Call to Repent (3:17-26)

Jesus had prayed, "Father, forgive them; for they know not what they do" (Luke 23:34). Peter faithfully reflects his Master's spirit when he says, "I know that you acted in ignorance, as did also your rulers." But ignorance is no longer an excuse. The clear fulfillment of the prophecy of the Suffering Servant ought to open everyone's eyes. "Repent," cries Peter. "Turn again, that your sins may be blotted out." He enforces his call in three principal ways.

The first has to do with the peculiar nature of the time in which he speaks. The time between Jesus' resurrection and his return has a special significance. During this period, Jesus is in heaven and the final End is delayed. This is the great opportunity to repent. On their face, Peter's words seem to mean that a great repentance of the Jewish nation would bring "times of refreshing" and hasten the return of Jesus as the Christ. This of course has not happened yet. But we still live between Jesus' resurrection and his return. This in-between time has lasted far longer than Peter thought it would. But its *quality* has not changed. This is still the age of repentance.

Peter's second argument for repentance (vss. 22 and 23) rests on the coming of the Prophet. In New Testament times, Moses was understood to have predicted, in Deuteronomy 18:15-19, the coming of a prophet like himself, one who would speak face to face with God. Moses had commanded Israel to heed that prophet and had pronounced destruction on those who would not listen. Peter implies that Jesus was that prophet. His hearers, who prided themselves on Moses but refused to listen to Jesus, must repent!

The third argument is based on the special privilege of his hearers. They live in the days of which all the prophets spoke. They are the sons of the prophets, the children of the Covenant. God's Servant has been sent to them first. This "sending" follows the Resurrection and refers not so much to Jesus' earthly ministry as to his presence in the Church which has now arisen in the midst of Israel.

Peter's sermon in Solomon's Porch shares with the sermon at Pentecost the basic points of the apostolic preaching: the fulfillment of prophecy and the dawn of the last days; the life, the death, the resurrection, and the exaltation of Jesus; the call to repent. Yet it is quite different in structure and in content. Although all the sermons are addressed to "Men of Israel," the impression grows that this sermon, more than any other, is an appeal to the Jewish nation for a national repentance. The strategic place in the Temple itself, the emphasis on the fathers, on Jewish guilt for the Crucifixion, on Abraham, Moses, Samuel, and all the prophets—all these contribute to this impression. In the earliest days the Christians dared to dream that the whole Jewish nation would repent and acknowledge Jesus as the Messiah. This hope never completely dies in Acts. But the whole course of the story from this point on shows Israel rejecting the gospel while the Gentiles, unexpectedly, accept it.

The Arrest of the Apostles (4:1-4)

Peter's sermon was broken off by the arrival of the Temple police. Even under Roman rule, the authority of the high priest within the Temple was unquestioned. Apparently he maintained an armed guard there, with its own captain. Some of the priests and other members of the Sadducee party came along. This was the very group which had engineered the arrest and execution of Jesus. They were provoked to find his disciples teaching in the very Temple itself and proclaiming in Jesus the resurrection of the dead.

This was a theological offense, for the Sadducees did not believe in the possibility of a resurrection. Even one exception would ruin their argument. But this was also dangerous teaching politically. It was bound to fan the popular belief that the general resurrection of all the dead was soon to come, and with it the overthrow of all Israel's enemies. This might lead to all sorts of uprisings and revolts against the established order. And the Sadducees did not want the established order changed. They were the small, powerful group who lined their pockets by co-operating with the Romans.

So they arrested Peter and John. It was too late for a trial that day, so they were kept in custody overnight. Perhaps the Sadducees hoped the arrest of the speakers would frighten the hearers and discredit what was said. It is a tribute to the power of the early preaching that a sermon which ended in arrest produced another harvest of converts. These new believers came in with their eyes open to the risk involved. There were now about five thousand in all.

Peter's Sermon to the Authorities (4:5-12)

The supreme court of the Jews was known as the Sanhedrin. It consisted of some seventy duly constituted members. Jesus had been tried before them; and now, as he had predicted (Mark 13:9), his followers stood at the same bar. The same men were there. Annas was the real power in the high-priestly family, although his son-in-law Caiaphas was technically recognized as high priest by the Romans. The John mentioned was, of course, not one of Jesus' disciples but another member of the high-priestly family. So was Alexander. These were the most powerful men in Jerusalem, men who worked closely with the Romans and who could expect their decisions to be backed by Roman troops.

Peter and John are ushered into the center of the room to face questioners on all sides of them. The question is phrased insultingly, as though to say: "By what sort of power and in what sort of name did you do this? Men like you!" Nowhere is the difference made by Pentecost more striking than in Peter's reply. A few months before, Peter had been afraid of the shadows of these men. Their servants had frightened him so that he denied his Master three times. But now, fully aware of what the same men might do to him, he flinches not at all. Filled with the Holy Spirit, he confesses his Lord and accuses his enemies to their faces.

What he says is not so much a defense as another sermon. It reviews the points made in Solomon's Portico: the power of the name to heal, the Crucifixion, and the Resurrection. But a new Scripture is brought in: Psalm 118. Jesus himself is reported to have used this Scripture with the same rulers (Luke 20:17). Here again, the full force of Peter's quotation can be felt only by reading the whole Psalm. "With the LORD on my side I do not fear. What can man do to me?" "In the name of the LORD"— thrice repeated. "I thank thee that thou hast answered me and hast become my salvation." These parts of the Psalm are surely in Peter's mind as well as the actual words quoted. But the center of interest is on the rejected stone. Peter equates the Jewish rulers with the builders in the Psalm, building the nation Israel.

Jesus is the stone they have rejected, as one that will not fit into their structure. But he has become the very cornerstone of a new Israel, the true one. Peter concludes by declaring that the power of Jesus' name, demonstrated in the healing, proves that salvation is in him and in him alone.

The Authorities Are at a Loss (4:13-22)

This unflinching and fluent reply to their question astounded the authorities. They had not expected this from simple Galilean fishermen. Particularly the use of the Old Testament amazed them. These men had not been schooled by the rabbis. They were laymen, not experts. The only explanation was that "they had been with Jesus." The rulers may have meant only that Jesus must have trained them during his ministry. But the true explanation which Luke intends his readers to understand is that they constantly sat at the feet of a Risen Lord who by his Spirit continued to open the Scriptures to them. Should this not be the aim of Christians today—to live so close to Christ that in moments of crisis even our enemies will be forced to the explanation that we have been with Jesus?

The difficulty of the authorities was further increased by the presence of the man formerly lame but now undoubtedly healed. At this point they sent the disciples and the healed man outside, so they could discuss the case freely. They saw that they had no case, for they could not deny the healing. So they resolved on a solemn warning.

They called the disciples and commanded them not to speak or teach at all in the name of Jesus. Peter and John stood their ground. God had commanded them to speak in this name. They would not stop. The rulers must judge whether men ought to listen to them rather than to God. This must have been infuriating to the authorities, but they felt powerless because of the general favor in which the Church was held by the mass of the people. They threatened them and let them go.

A Remarkable Prayer Meeting (4:23-31)

Before Pentecost the threats of the rulers would have driven the disciples into despair and hiding. Now they are the occasion of a joyous prayer meeting. Corporate prayer had been a custom of the group ever since the days of waiting in the Upper Room (see 1:14, 24; 2:42, 47), whether in the Temple or in homes.

But this is the first time Acts indicates what these prayers were like.

The beginning is typical of Jewish prayers of the day, as we would expect. Then the Second Psalm is quoted. It is applied to the gathering of Jesus' enemies in Jerusalem. But what those enemies did was made a part of God's predestined purpose. Even so, the argument runs, whatever these enemies may do to us can only further God's purpose in Christ. Here is a faith with which to meet threats!

The petition of the prayer is not for protection but for boldness. They do not ask to be excused from proclaiming the offensive name; they ask for more healings, more signs and wonders. Twice in the prayer Jesus is called God's holy servant. The name they proclaim belongs to the Suffering One, and they rejoice that they, too, can suffer. The idea that the Church is to continue Jesus' mission as God's Suffering Servant is never a welcome thought. Does this have anything to do with the Church's lack of power and of boldness?

The prayer was followed by a great upsurge of spiritual power. The place was shaken. They were all filled with the Holy Spirit. Some interpreters have seen in this a parallel account of the Pentecost experience. Both stories do tell of physical disturbances and of a whole company being filled with the Holy Spirit. But after the initial outpouring there were many subsequent experiences of the power of the Spirit, both in the whole group and in the individual members of it. Although Pentecost itself—the initial giving of the Spirit to the Church—is an unrepeatable event, a new release of the Spirit's power, like the one recorded here, ought to be possible in our own day.

Greed Dramatically Punished (4:32—5:11)

All Things in Common (4:32-35)

Here is another of Luke's general descriptions of life in the Early Church. It is similar to 2:43-47. The verbs are in the same tense of continuous action, yet certain different emphases appear. After a reminder that believers had everything in common, Luke stresses the spiritual gifts which accompanied the testimony of the Apostles to the Resurrection. *Power* was a mark of their preaching. This is the word which describes the miracles of Jesus. Just as his words had the power to still storms and heal the sick, so the preaching of the Apostles did things; it moved men. And *grace* was on them all. This is not the later theological sense of the word: God's undeserved favor. It is the early meaning: winsomeness, attractiveness. The common life of the Early Church fascinated and drew people. Luke then returns to the sharing of goods and adds this significant detail: men were even moved to sell real estate—houses and lands—and to lay the proceeds at the Apostles' feet.

This is a good place to analyze in detail the so-called "communism" of the Early Church. It was not unique. There were other groups in the first century who practiced a community of goods. This was a marked feature of the Covenanters of the Dead Sea Scrolls community. To enter that community, a man had to turn all his property over to be administered by the heads of the organization. But the sharing of wealth in the Early Church was different in several ways.

First of all, private property was not formally abolished. The people gave what was their own. To abolish private possession is to abolish giving, since a man can give only what is his. Second, the sharing was voluntary, not forced. It was not a condition of entrance into the Church. A man might say, "What I possess is not my own." But no one said to him, "What you possess is ours."

In sum, the material sharing of goods was simply a natural outward consequence of a deep inner sharing in the Holy Spirit. Jesus had instituted some kind of sharing among his disciples, for there was a common purse which Judas had kept. He had suggested to the rich young ruler and others that they sell what they had and give to the poor. It was only natural that the Early Church, so keenly aware that in the Spirit Jesus continued to dwell in their midst, should take his commands quite literally. If I have more than I need, and a brother who shares with me in the Spirit is in want, it is unthinkable for me to hold selfishly what I have. This is the root of the so-called "communism" of the Early Church.

Was the sharing of goods ultimately a failure? Human weakness soon abused it, as we shall see (5:1-11). After Acts 6 we hear no more of it in its primitive form. It may have been economic foolishness, impractical in a corrupt world. The community could not have continued to live indefinitely by liquidating capital. Someone has said it was an ideal system only if society were coming to an end or capital were not. But it was spiritually significant. The economic order has changed many times since the first century, but we may still ask ourselves if Christian fellowship is real when it does not affect the things we possess. The best commentaries on this are I John 3:17-18 and James 2:15-16.

The Example of Barnabas (4:36-37)

Luke now turns, as he often does, from a general description to particular incidents. First he tells briefly of Barnabas, who sold a field and gave his money to be distributed to the needy in the Church. Barnabas is one of the most lovable characters in Acts, always quick to appreciate the good in others, very unselfish, and not desirous of his own glory. He appears here as an example of all that was good in the voluntary sharing of the Early Church.

The Death of Ananias and Sapphira (5:1-11)

The story of Ananias is a direct contrast to that of Barnabas. Probably because he envied the praise that Barnabas had received for his generosity, he too sold some property. But he was not willing to give all the proceeds to the Church. With his wife's consent, he kept back part. Then in direct imitation of Barnabas, he laid the money at the Apostles' feet. Peter's words make it quite clear that Ananias' sin was deceit. He wanted the credit for sacrificial giving without making the sacrifice. His pretending to give all was the sin; he was under no requirement to give all.

Peter declared that such an attempt to deceive the Church is a lie to the Holy Spirit himself. Ananias fell down and died. The death of Ananias is sometimes described as a "miracle of destruction." But there is no curse in the story as it stands. There is no indication that Peter willed his death. The condemnation struck home. The guilt of what he had done sank in. The terrifying thought that he had lied to the Holy Spirit was too much for him. So he died.

We are not told why Ananias was buried without Sapphira's knowing of his death. Many details of the story are puzzling. Peter by a question learned that Sapphira was a partner in her husband's fraud. He accused her of the same crime: tempting the Spirit of the Lord. In this case, he predicted her punishment: "The feet of those that have buried your husband are at the door, and they will carry you out." The shock was too much for her, and soon she too was buried. Small wonder that all who heard it were afraid.

The story of Ananias and Sapphira is disturbing. Some have felt that those who handed down the story imposed on it an interpretation that was not altogether in harmony with the spirit of Jesus. Yet it was like him to be more stern with "decent" sins than with the sins of the flesh. And no one has ever denounced covetousness more strongly than he. We should be cautious in rejecting this story. It is a sobering thought that the severest punishment that occurred in the primitive Church did not fall on a murderer or a thief. It fell on a "respectable" couple, who falsified their Church pledge in order to appear generous when they were really greedy.

Persecution by the Authorities (5:12-42)

Signs and Wonders of the Apostles (5:12-16)

Once again Luke gives a general description of the state of the Church (see 2:43-47 and 4:32-35). This time the emphasis falls in a special way upon the Apostles and upon the signs and wonders done by them.

There seems to be a contradiction between verse 13, where no one dares to join the Christians, and verse 14, where multitudes of men and women are added to the Lord. A possible solution is that "the rest" in verse 13 refers to the elders and leaders of the Jews, in contrast with the common people who held the Christians in high honor and joined them in increasing numbers.

The reverence of the common people for the Apostles reached actual superstition. They hoped that Peter's shadow would heal the sick. It is hard to believe that Peter encouraged this (see Acts 3:12). It is told simply to illustrate the awe which the Church and its leaders inspired in the common people.

A Second Brush with the Law (5:17-26)

A story which follows is very much like the story of Peter and John before the rulers (Acts 4:1-31). In both stories there is an arrest at the end of the day, a night in jail, a sermon by Peter, a warning from the rulers, a refusal to obey, release, and renewed enthusiasm in the Church. Some interpreters have felt that we have two records of one arrest. Yet it is certainly neither impossible nor improbable that Christian leaders were arrested more than once. And there are striking differences in the second story. It is in this second brush with the law that the first blood is drawn —by stinging whips on the bare backs of the Apostles.

The growing influence of the Apostles on the mass of the Jewish people filled the high priest and his party with furious jealousy. This time all of the Apostles were arrested and put in jail. But an angel of the Lord opened the prison doors and told them to return to the Temple and preach "all the words of this Life." The gospel conveys not just a new moral code, not just a new explanation of things, but Life!

We do not need to imagine a shining being with feathery wings unlocking the doors. The word "angel" means "messenger" or "agent." In many stories in the Old Testament, the "angel of the Lord" is an expression for God's intervention in human affairs (see, for example, Isa. 37:36, where what was probably a destructive plague is called "the angel of the LORD"). As in the Old Israel, so in the New: God himself intervenes to deliver and instruct his servants. The details are not given.

In the meanwhile, the Sanhedrin (see the comment on 4:5-12) had been assembled to try the Apostles. The escape of the prisoners caused great confusion. But since they had not run away but had obediently returned to their post in the Temple, they were soon found and brought, without violence, before the supreme court of the Jews.

A Second Sermon to the Authorities (5:27-32)

The high priest came immediately to the point. His warning, issued in Acts 4:18, had been disobeyed. The people were coming to blame him and his party for Jesus' death.

Peter's answer is shorter than in the first trial, but is the same in all essentials. Once again he declares that it is necessary to obey God rather than human authority, when the two conflict (compare 5:29 with 4:19). There are limits on the Christian's duty to the state. This is a point that needs careful study and interpretation in our own day.

The constant themes of the apostolic preaching ring out here: the Crucifixion, the Resurrection, the exaltation of Jesus to God's right hand, the call to repentance, and the offer of forgiveness. Notice that the Holy Spirit, as well as the Apostles, is a witness of these things. His presence in the Church is the strongest evidence for Christ's position at God's right hand.

In all this, Peter makes no apology for laying the blame for
Jesus' death on the Sanhedrin. He repeats that this is the plain
truth of the matter: "whom you killed by hanging him on a tree."

Gamaliel's Counsel (5:33-39)

Peter's sermon was not calculated to win friends and influence
people. His words cut the priest and his party like the teeth of a
saw, says the Greek. The Apostles would probably have been
executed that very day if a member of the Sanhedrin named
Gamaliel had not come to their defense. Gamaliel was one of
the most famous teachers of the day, a learned and greatly hon-
ored man. As a Pharisee, he was a natural opponent of the Sadducees.

After the prisoners had been taken out of the court, Gamaliel
reviewed two attempted revolutions that had miserably failed because God was not with them. There is considerable difficulty
about the illustrations in Gamaliel's speech. According to secular
records, the revolution of Theudas occurred after that of Judas.
Indeed, it occurred after Gamaliel's speech. Perhaps there was
more than one Theudas. Our records of the period are too fragmentary to enable us to be sure of the solution to this problem.
But the main point Gamaliel makes is quite clear: Let these men
alone; if God is not with them, they will fail; if he is, you cannot
stop them. Is this good advice for problems before the Church
today?

Beaten for the Name (5:40-42)

Gamaliel's advice prevailed: the Apostles were not executed.
They were given a second warning. But the Sadducees were too
angry to let them go with words only. The Apostles were stripped
to the waist and beaten with whips. The Greek word resembles
our English expression: "to take the skin off" someone. Jesus had
endured the same punishment (see Luke 22:63).

The reaction of the Apostles is noteworthy. They were not
cowed or discouraged. In the very face of the Sanhedrin, as they
were leaving, they began to rejoice. Joy in suffering is an authentic New Testament experience (see I Peter 4:13; James 1:2; Phil.
1:29; Col. 1:24). All suffering was to be borne patiently, but suffering "for the name"—for the sake of Jesus and after the example of Jesus—was an occasion for thanksgiving and joy.

The warning of the Sanhedrin was not obeyed. The Apostles

continued their witness to Jesus in the two customary centers, the Temple and private homes. In their teaching and their preaching, there was one great theme: Jesus is the Christ. Is the Church today easily silenced when its message proves to be unpopular? Does the Church today rejoice in suffering for the name, or avoid it at all costs?

Disunity Leads to Organization (6:1-6)

The Problem (6:1)

The larger the Church grew, the harder it became to maintain the warm, free fellowship that marked it at the beginning. In the sharing of goods, some system had to replace occasional spontaneous acts of generosity. So a daily distribution of food, and perhaps of other necessities, was begun. Such distribution was an established principle among Jewish synagogues. Before long, this led to a bitter dispute. Two factions emerged in the Church, the Hellenists and the Hebrews. The Hellenists charged that the widows in their group were being neglected in the daily distribution.

Unfortunately, we have no further clue as to who the Hellenists and the Hebrews were, and there is considerable disagreement on this point. The simplest explanation, in the light of our present knowledge, seems to be that both groups were Jewish Christians. The Hebrews were strict Jews, typified by the Pharisees whom we know so well from the Gospels. The Hellenists were also Jews, but they did not live according to the orthodox Jewish customs. The word "Hellenist" means one who lives as a Greek. In what respect these men lived more like Greeks than Jews we are not told. More must have been involved than language, for Paul, who spoke Greek, calls himself "a Hebrew born of Hebrews" (Phil. 3:5). It has recently been suggested that there is a connection between the sect that produced the Dead Sea Scrolls and the Hellenists.

The Solution (6:2-6)

In the face of this threat to the unity of the Church, the Apostles took immediate action. Seven new church officers, who would take responsibility for the distribution, were elected and installed.

The election has several points of interest. The Apostles set the number at seven and laid down the qualifications: "of good repute, full of the Spirit and of wisdom." But the whole congregation elected. There is no mention of the use of lots. The Apostles then inducted them into their office by prayer and the laying on of hands (see also 8:17; 9:17; 13:3; 19:6).

It is notable that all seven of the men chosen bear Greek names. Possibly the Hebrews, in the generosity which should mark Christians in a dispute, saw to it that all seven were Hellenists. One was even a "proselyte"—a Gentile who had become a Jew.

What office were these men given? Often they are called the first deacons. It is true that the verb "to serve" (Acts 6:2) is in Greek "to deacon," and the noun "ministry" (Acts 6:4) is in Greek "deaconing." But the word "deacon" itself is not used here. And the work done later by Stephen and Philip was more like the work of the Apostles than like the work of deacons in most modern churches. It is probably better to think of the seven as being a unique group, like the Twelve, and not a permanent order in the Church.

Stephen, the First Martyr (6:7—8:3)

The Growth of the Church (6:7)

Luke's summary here (compare 2:43-47; 4:32-35; and 5:12-16) is very brief, but well worth noticing. Here the growth of the Church is described as an increase of "the word of God." It is a striking figure. It is the Word of God which calls the Church into being, and it is by hearing and obeying that Word that the Church grows. Here, too, we have the only record of converts from among the priests.

Stephen Falsely Accused (6:8-15)

Stephen, one of the seven, now takes the center of the stage. The Holy Spirit had bestowed upon him exceptional gifts (6:5, 8, 10, 15). Also, the Spirit had led him further than others into an understanding of what Christianity really involved. These new and revolutionary ideas aroused opposition in certain synagogues in Jerusalem. Cilicia (see vs. 9) was the home of Saul, who later became the Apostle Paul, and it is possible that he was among Stephen's hearers. When they could not best him in argument, his opponents raised a cry of blasphemy, stirred up a mob, and brought him before the Sanhedrin.

Stephen was accused of attacking the Temple and the Law. False witnesses quoted him as saying that Jesus of Nazareth would destroy the Temple. It is singular that this is the exact charge brought against Jesus himself by false witnesses (see Mark 14:57-59). What Jesus really said is summarized for us in John 2:19. Possibly Stephen had tried to quote Jesus and had been misunderstood, even as Jesus himself was misunderstood.

The Fathers of Israel (7:1-8)

When Stephen is permitted to speak, he does not answer the charges directly, but sets forth his theology in the form of a review of Israel's history. Notice throughout the speech how often God is the subject of the sentences. To Stephen, the history of Israel is the history of the acts of God.

God's first great act was the call of Abraham. Stephen stresses the fact that this act did not take place on the sacred soil of Palestine, but in Mesopotamia, in the land of the Chaldeans. Here, and throughout the speech, Stephen is summarizing the main drive of the Old Testament from memory. The details are not so important to him, and seeming contradictions arise. For example, Genesis 12:1-3 places Abraham's call at Haran rather than in the land of the Chaldeans. But surely God was dealing with Abraham before he moved to Haran. This is understood in Genesis 15:7, where God says: "I am the LORD who brought you from Ur of the Chaldeans."

After Abraham entered the land of promise, he had no real possession of it, nor did the other patriarchs: Isaac, Jacob, and Jacob's twelve sons. Stephen is attacking the idea that the true Israel is tied to "this land in which you are now living." The fathers worshiped God and had a covenant with him quite apart from possessing the land.

The Story of Joseph (7:9-16)

Here we encounter a second great theme of Stephen's speech. The history of Israel is the story not only of God's gracious acts, but also of Israel's outrageous rejection of those whom God sent to deliver them. Thus the fathers, of whom the Jews were so proud, sold Joseph, their future deliverer, into slavery. But God acted again, this time on Egyptian soil, to rescue Joseph and prepare him to deliver Israel. The result was that the fathers died, not in the land of promise, but in a foreign land.

Here again there are minor differences in detail between Stephen's account and the Old Testament record. They disagree on how many persons went down into Egypt (compare Acts 7:14 with Exod. 1:5); on who purchased the cave at Shechem (compare Acts 7:16 and Gen. 33:19); and on who was buried there (compare Acts 7:16 and Gen. 49:29-32). Stephen's copy of the Old Testament was undoubtedly in the Septuagint translation, in which the numbers often differ from the Hebrew original. The matter of the cave is more difficult, and even Calvin admits bluntly that either Stephen, Luke, or a copyist has made a mistake.

The Story of Moses (7:17-43)

The heart of Stephen's speech is a moving interpretation of the story of Moses. Like Joseph, Moses was rejected by his brethren, who did not accept him as God's deliverer (7:23-29). But God acted again, this time in the land of Midian, revealing himself in the burning bush. Expressly it is said that the place was holy ground (7:33).

To this one whom Israel had rejected was given the honor of leading Israel out of Egypt and of receiving the Law at Mount Sinai. Yet even after this, the fathers rejected him again, sought to return to Egypt, made the golden calf, and became idolaters.

In Stephen's interpretation, this was the crucial turning point in Israel's history. The rejection of Moses, God's deliverer, led to a rejection of God himself. The essence of God's promise to Abraham's seed was that they should return from bondage to worship him (7:7). But because of the rebellion in the wilderness, they were given over to idolatry instead. As evidence of their idolatry from the forty years in the wilderness on, Stephen quotes Amos 5:25-27. Quoting from memory, under the stress of great emotion, he changes the prophecy in a few details.

In Stephen's account of Moses we find not so much contradictions of the Old Testament narrative as additions to it. Most of them are such as a reverent imagination would supply. In two cases, Stephen seems to be drawing on oral traditions that were popular among the Jews of his day: (1) That Moses' life fell into three periods of forty years each (see 7:23, 30); and (2) that the Law was given through the mediation of angels (7:38; compare 7:53; Gal. 3:19; and Hebrews 2:2).

The Inadequacy of the Temple (7:44-50)

By his repeated stress on the acts of God outside of Palestine, Stephen has already been undermining the superstitious idea held by many Jews that the *Shekinah,* the real presence of God, could be found only in the Temple at Jerusalem. Now he turns from the ancient heroes of Israel and centers on the Temple itself. The Tent of Witness, the Tabernacle, had been an adequate place of worship in the glorious days of Moses, Joshua, and David. Solomon did build a Temple, but the prophets criticized it, saying that other gods may be thought to dwell in such houses, but not the Most High.

"You Stiff-Necked People" (7:51-53)

Suddenly Stephen breaks off and attacks directly. One can almost imagine he was goaded by a heckler. The object of his attack is Israel. Israel's whole history is resistance against the Holy Spirit. The prophets who spoke by the Spirit have been persecuted and killed. And now this generation has betrayed the Righteous One himself. The Righteous One is God's Suffering Servant (see the comment on Acts 3:11-16). Stephen's smashing climax reminds us of Jesus' words in Luke 11:47-51 and the parable of the Vineyard (Luke 20:9-18). Only in his last few words does Stephen meet definitely the accusation that he had spoken against the Law. It is not the Law that he attacks but Israel's failure to keep it.

Stephen's Theology

Stephen broke off before he could round out his argument. He drew no logical conclusions, and he suggested far more than he said. We need to do our best to understand what he was driving at.

It seems clear that Joseph and Moses and the prophets are introduced as "types" of Jesus; that is, their stories parallel his in strangely significant ways. As they were God's deliverers for Israel, so was he. As Israel rejected them, so they rejected him. This is stressed in the case of Moses, whose word about the coming of a prophet *like himself* is quoted here as a prediction (7:37).

In the same way, the golden calf seems to be a "type" of the Temple. The calf was a work of their own hands (compare 7:41 with 7:48). It became an object of idolatrous worship. This, Stephen intimates, is what the Temple has become.

To what practical effects does such a theology point? It convicts Israel of a long history of rebellion against God, reaching its climax in the judicial murder of the Righteous One himself. Clearly Israel must repent or forfeit forever her position as God's Chosen People. This theology also intimates that God could have a people in lands other than Palestine and be worshiped in places other than the Temple.

Here we have the conception of a Christianity which was not a part of Judaism. The ideas which bore fruit in the mind of Paul, and resulted in the foundation of Gentile churches, were present in germ in Stephen's mind.

In a way Stephen's enemies understood him well enough. He was a threat to the Temple and the Law. The threat affected their pocketbooks, since the Temple was the main source of income, directly or indirectly, for all Jerusalem. And it affected their religious pride, since the Law was what set them apart from the Gentiles. A theology which threatened those two things was intolerable.

Stephen Is Stoned (7:54—8:3)

Stephen's direct attack "sawed through" his hearers (see the comment on 5:33). They ground their teeth in uncontrollable rage. At this moment, when he stood condemned before a human court, Stephen was granted by the Spirit a vision of the heavenly court. He saw Jesus, the Son of Man, not seated at God's right hand to exercise rule and authority, but standing at God's right hand to give testimony in behalf of his witness on earth. Surely the promise of Luke 12:8 was in his mind.

When Stephen reported his vision, the Sanhedrin and the spectators at the trial could stand it no longer. It is difficult to determine whether what followed was mob action or a legal execution. The loud cries, the stopped ears, and the rush of the crowd upon him (vs. 57) all sound like a lynching party. But the care taken to move outside the city, so its sacredness would not be polluted, and the presence of witnesses (vs. 58), show at least a semblance of legal procedure. The execution of Stephen could have been justified, in the mind of the Sanhedrin, by Leviticus 24:10-16; Deuteronomy 13:6-11; or Deuteronomy 17:2-7. The prescribed method was stoning, in which the condemned man was thrown over a cliff and finished off by rolling large stones down upon him. Why was not the consent of the Romans necessary, as it had been in the execution of Jesus? Two explanations are possible. There was a period in A.D. 36, just after Pilate was dismissed, when there was no effective Roman rule in Jerusalem. Possibly the martyrdom of Stephen took place then. The other explanation is to take the view that Stephen's trial was interrupted by a lynch mob which sought no permission from anyone. Pilate, whose headquarters were in Caesarea except during the feasts, had no chance to interfere.

In his death, Stephen resembled his Lord. Compare his last words with those of Jesus: Acts 7:59 with Luke 23:46, and Acts 7:60 with Luke 23:34. Luke is able to describe his death, amid the crashing stones, in the words "he fell asleep." There are few more striking illustrations in Scripture of how Jesus' victory over death robbed it of its sting for his followers.

Stephen died an apparent failure. So far as human eye could see, he had convinced neither friend nor enemy that Christianity could not remain tied to the Temple and the Law of Moses. Moreover, he had brought to an end the popularity which Christianity had enjoyed with the mass of the Jewish people (see 2:47; 4:21; 5:13, 26). Now for the first time a general persecution arose against the Church. Many of the believers had to flee from the city to the surrounding districts of Judea and Samaria. The Apostles managed to remain in Jerusalem, perhaps by "going underground." Apparently it was too risky for his fellow believers even to bury Stephen, and the task was left to devout Jews (burying the dead was a very important part of Jewish piety).

But "God moves in a mysterious way his wonders to perform." If it had not been for this general persecution, the Church might have remained a small sect in Jerusalem, ignoring the missionary command of her Lord. Now the disciples were forced into the second stage: the witness "in all Judea and Samaria" (see 1:8). As for the new truth which Stephen had tried to proclaim, it had found root in most unlikely soil. Stephen had no way of knowing that every word he said had been branded on the conscience of a young Pharisee from Tarsus named Saul. Saul would never forget Stephen's face (see 6:15). He would never forget his dying prayers. He would never forget that the witnesses had laid their garments at his feet or that he had approved of Stephen's execution (see Acts 22:20). Saul was destined to become the Apostle Paul. Augustine understood Acts when he wrote: "The Church owes Paul to the prayers of Stephen." For the time being, however, Saul's guilty conscience drove him to take the lead in persecuting the Church.

THE WITNESS IN JUDEA AND SAMARIA

Acts 8:4—12:23

The Ministry of Philip (8:4-40)

Philip and the Samaritans (8:4-13)

As he so often does, Luke follows a general statement (that the scattered believers went about preaching the word) with a typical example (the story of Philip). One of Jesus' twelve Apostles was named Philip, but it is far more natural to suppose that this Philip was a companion of Stephen, one of the seven (see 6:5).

To escape the persecution, which must have been particularly severe against Stephen's close friends, Philip fled to a city of Samaria. Samaria was the region, lying between Judea on the south and Galilee on the north, where the Samaritans lived.

In Old Testament times it had been the heart-land of the Northern Kingdom, the most famous and prosperous part of the country. When the Assyrians carried the leaders of the Northern Kingdom into captivity, they imported foreigners to take their place. These foreigners intermarried with the poorer Israelites who remained, and a mixed religion resulted (see II Kings 17:24-41). They were later called Samaritans. Years later when the people of the Southern Kingdom had also been conquered, carried captive, and permitted to return, the Samaritans opposed the rebuilding of Jerusalem. Intense hatred developed in the days of Nehemiah. The Samaritans withdrew and built their own temple on Mount Gerizim.

This intense hatred continued to the time of Jesus. The Jews had no dealings with Samaritans. Jesus shocked his contemporaries by talking with a Samaritan woman (see John 4) and by making a Samaritan the hero of one of his most beautiful parables (see Luke 10:29-37).

Now Philip, finding himself among the Samaritans, did not hesitate to proclaim to them that the Messiah had come. And when they believed, he did not hesitate to receive them into the

Church by baptism (see vs. 12). This was a startling break in a deeply set racial pattern. What led Philip to make it? Perhaps he shared Stephen's views. Perhaps he was influenced by the attitude Jesus had shown toward the Samaritans. At any rate, the results proved that he was being led by the Holy Spirit.

One man in the city was unhappy over this. His name was Simon. He was a magician, and by his tricks he had persuaded the Samaritans that he possessed divine powers. Now his position of power and prestige was undermined. Even his self-confidence was shattered as he saw signs and miracles he could not duplicate with his magic. Simon was baptized as a believer, though it soon became evident that his faith was imperfect.

The Apostles Come to Investigate (8:14-25)

Communication was somehow maintained with the Apostles, who had stuck it out in Jerusalem while the persecution raged. They were naturally concerned that one of the Hellenist leaders had moved so far so fast, venturing to open up a whole new territory to the gospel, in defiance of time-honored prejudices and traditions. Peter and John were sent to investigate. To their great credit, they did not block this new movement of the Spirit, but co-operated with it.

The interesting statement is made here that though the Samaritans had been baptized in the name of the Lord Jesus, they still needed to receive the Holy Spirit. Here there is an apparent separation between water-baptism and Spirit-baptism. We can understand how the two experiences were separate for the original Apostles, who received their water-baptism from John the Baptist and their Spirit-baptism on the Day of Pentecost. But in the days following Pentecost—and that includes our own day—do these baptisms remain separate and distinct? Or were we correct in understanding Peter's words at Pentecost to mean that the two now normally belong together? (See the comment on Acts 2:37-40.)

There are three instances in Acts where the two baptisms seem to be separate. The other two concern Cornelius (10:44-48) and the disciples at Ephesus (19:1-7). In all the other baptisms recorded, there is no mention of a separate baptism of the Spirit. These three cases are clearly the exception, not the rule. We need, however, to try to understand them.

In this case, there were abundant evidences of the Spirit's presence in Samaria already. The power of Philip's preaching, the

signs and wonders which he performed, the great joy that spread
through the city—these things are commonly considered gifts of
the Spirit in the New Testament.

It was not, then, that the Spirit was altogether lacking. Rather,
some signal gift which the early believers regarded as *the* sign of
the Spirit had not come. What was this gift? It was something so
definite and sensational that Simon could see it happen (8:18).
Almost surely it was the gift of speaking with tongues. That had
been the most sensational feature on the Day of Pentecost (see
the comment on 2:4), and new converts would naturally desire
it. The expression in verse 16—"for it had not yet fallen on any
of them"—is language appropriate to the sudden outburst of in-
coherent, exalted speech (compare 10:44-46; 11:15).

Whatever it was, the gift of the Spirit came to the Samaritans
when the Apostles prayed and laid their hands on them. Does
this mean that only Apostles can convey the Spirit? If so, did the
Ethiopian eunuch never receive the Spirit; since, after Philip baptized him, no Apostle laid hands on him? (8:26-40). And was
Ananias an apostle since, when he laid his hands on Saul, Saul
did receive the Spirit? (9:10-19). On the other hand, does this
mean that the Spirit is given by the laying on of hands (which in
some churches has become a sacred rite, called "confirmation"),
rather than by baptism? If so, why is no mention made of it in
the story of Pentecost and elsewhere?

Belief on the "name" of Jesus, baptism, the laying on of hands,
and the reception of the Holy Spirit are all ideas of tremendous
importance in Acts, and they are all closely connected. But when
we seek to discover the exact connection, we are baffled.

This is reflected in the confusion of the Church today over
baptism, confirmation, and "the apostolic succession." This much
seems certain: that the essential significance of both baptism and
the laying on of hands was vital connection with the Church, the
body of believers; and that to those who became vitally connected, the Spirit, who was at work in the body of believers, ex-
tended his gifts.

To return to the story, the Apostles prayed; they laid their
hands on the Samaritans; the Samaritans began to speak with
tongues. Simon was amazed. In his interpretation the Spirit was
a magic genie, a power that could be controlled by the fortunate
men who were his masters. Here was a chance to obtain *real*
magical powers, to restore his lost prestige and authority quickly

and sensationally. So he offered the Apostles money in exchange
for the power to manipulate the Holy Spirit. Peter's rebuke was
swift and severe. Such an offer revealed a complete and total mis-
understanding of the Holy Spirit, and a heart full of iniquity.
Simon was frightened and begged the Apostles' prayers. The
Bible tells us nothing more of Simon, though he figures in later
traditions as an archenemy of the Christian faith.

A lesson often drawn from this story is that to buy offices in
the Church is wicked. This sin is called simony. But there is a far
deeper lesson here. The Holy Spirit is not power to be manipu-
lated, but power to be obeyed. He is not a genie whom we command. He is Lord and commands us. Simon thought that the
Spirit came to Samaria in obedience to the Apostles. On the contrary, the Apostles went to Samaria, and received the despised
Samaritans into the Church, in obedience to the Spirit. And they
continued to obey as they stopped to evangelize other Samaritan
villages on the way back to Jerusalem.

The Ethiopian Eunuch (8:26-40)

Luke relates a second incident from the ministry of Philip. In
obedience to the angel of the Lord (see the comment on 5:17-
21), Philip went out on the highway that led to Egypt and met the
Ethiopian eunuch. Three questions are often raised about this interesting figure: (1) Was he a Negro? In answering this, we must
distinguish between modern Ethiopia and ancient Ethiopia. The
rulers of modern Ethiopia (formerly Abyssinia) are the Ax-
umites, a Semitic people who came originally from the Arabian
peninsula. But in New Testament times, the word Ethiopia indi-
cated an ancient kingdom, with its capital at Meroë, in what is
now the Sudan. Its people were Nubians, black-skinned people of
African descent. (2) Was he literally a eunuch? Officials who
served queens often were. Yet in Egypt the word was used, without its literal meaning, for any high court official. A definite answer is impossible. (3) Was he a proselyte, that is, a Gentile who
had officially become a Jew? The fact that he made the long
journey to worship at Jerusalem points in this direction. However, it is more likely that he belonged to the large group of
"God-fearers"; that is, Gentiles who had been strongly attracted
to Judaism, who studied the Scriptures, worshiped in the Court
of the Gentiles, attended the synagogues, but who had not become.
Jews.

The eunuch traveled by chariot (here a covered carriage, not a war chariot), as was fitting for the treasurer of a great queen. Philip, at the Spirit's command, overtook him by running, and heard him reading from the fifty-third chapter of Isaiah. Interestingly, in ancient times people seem to have read aloud, even when reading to themselves! At the eunuch's invitation, Philip rode with him and proclaimed to him the good news that Jesus had fulfilled this prophecy, that he was God's Suffering Servant, and that he had been "taken up from the earth" to reign as Lord. This is the most direct application of Isaiah 53 to Jesus in the New Testament. But the multitude of other references show that this chapter was focal in the understanding of the early preachers and of Jesus himself (see Matt. 8:17; Mark 10:45; 14:24; Luke 22:37; 24:26, 46; John 1:29; 12:38; Acts 3:13-14, 26; 4:27, 30; 7:52; Rom. 4:25; 10:16; Heb. 9:28; I Peter 2:22-25).

The eunuch willingly accepted the gospel and asked to be baptized. Verse 37 (see margin) is not found in the best manuscripts, but it is evidence of the simple confession of faith required of early converts. Verses 38 and 39 shed some light on the disputed question of the method of baptism in the Early Church. Clearly both Philip and the eunuch went down and stood in the pool or stream. It is still not clear, however, whether Philip poured water over the eunuch or immersed him. Baptism with the Spirit accompanied the baptism with water. Both men were lifted out of themselves: Philip hardly knew where he was until he reached Azotus; the eunuch, when he came to himself, found Philip gone, but the Spirit's gift of joy stayed with him as he journeyed homeward. Philip continued his missionary work and settled in Caesarea.

The Conversion of Saul (9:1-30)

The Damascus Road (9:1-9)

The missionary work of Philip was one of the sequels to Stephen's martyrdom. The conversion of Saul was another. Unable to forget Stephen, Saul transferred his guilt into hostility against all the disciples of the Lord and tried to silence his conscience by feverish activity. The church at Jerusalem had been forced underground, but refugees were reported to have reached Damascus and there was danger that the Way was spreading there also. "The Way" seems to have been the name given to the Christian faith by the Jews, in derision (see 19:9, 23; 22:4; 24:14, 22). But Christianity was in truth the Way. As the prophet had foretold, God had done a new thing and made a new "way" for his people (Isa. 40:3-5; 42:15-17; 43:19). Accepting the taunt of the Jews, the Church eagerly proclaimed the Way (see Mark 1:1-4; John 14:3-6). But to Saul, the Way was an ugly heresy, to be stamped out at all costs. Armed with letters from the high priest, he set out for Damascus. Damascus had a large Jewish population. Not only was orthodox Judaism represented there by many synagogues, but a colony of the same group who wrote the Dead Sea Scrolls was there also. Perhaps the latter were among the first to join the Way.

The journey of several days gave Paul time to think, and he was inwardly in turmoil as he neared Damascus itself. Suddenly he had a tremendous religious experience: he saw a very bright light, fell to the ground, and heard a voice. The experience left him blinded and without desire for food and drink for three days. The fact that his companions did not share fully in this experience (9:7; compare 22:9) does not mean it was not completely real to Paul. It was the turning point of his life (see Gal. 1:15-16; I Cor. 9:1; 15:8). There have been many, many times since when men have seen lights, heard voices, and fallen senseless at the time of conversion. Yet it is a mistake to feel that these things are essentials of conversion.

The essentials are these: Saul recognized that Jesus, whom he was persecuting, was Lord—he was the one to whom life must be surrendered from this moment on; and Saul began to obey this new Lord in so far as he understood his will. These two points remain clear, even if the familiar question, "Lord, what wilt thou have me to do?", must be omitted in accordance with the best manuscripts (but see 22:10). Every genuine conversion has these essentials at its heart. It is interesting to notice that in Saul's conversion experience Jesus identifies himself with his persecuted Church. Saul had been persecuting the little band of believers; the voice says: "Why do you persecute *me?*" Some students think that Paul's conception of the Church as "the body of Christ" had its beginning here on the Damascus road.

The Visit of Ananias (9:10-19)

Ananias (not to be confused with the Ananias of Acts 5:1-11) may have been a refugee from the Jerusalem church, but if he

had only heard of the persecutions (vs. 13) he was more likely
a native of Damascus, recently converted. It is not remarkable
that he at first resisted the Lord's command that he go and help
the archenemy of all believers. But it is truly remarkable that
when he did go, he addressed him as "Brother Saul." The hard
sayings of Jesus about loving one's enemies and doing good to
one's persecutors (Luke 6:27-36) were already bearing fruit. To
this word of Ananias, as well as to Stephen's prayers, the Church
owes the Apostle Paul.

Through the loving hands of Ananias, Paul's sight was restored.
Notice here that the laying on of hands (*not* by an Apostle)
precedes baptism; that baptism follows immediately, apparently
right in the house; that the Spirit is given without additional steps
or ceremonies.

Saul in Damascus and Jerusalem (9:20-30)

With characteristic energy, Saul immediately began to preach
his new-found faith. He began in Damascus a pattern which was
to mark his entire ministry. He preached first to the Jews in the
synagogues. Using the Old Testament Scriptures he sought to
persuade them that Jesus was the Messiah, the Son of God.

To the loyal Jews in Damascus, this was the last straw. Saul
had not carried out the task for which he had volunteered; he
had made no arrests; now he was lending his superior talents to
the support of the hated Way. They made a plot to kill him, and
watched the city gates to prevent his escape. But Saul's disciples,
those whom he himself had converted, let him down over the wall
in a basket.

Saul then returned to Jerusalem. Quite naturally the disciples,
who had suffered so much from him, distrusted his claims that
he was now a believer. They took him for a spy. But Barnabas
(see the comment on 4:36-37) believed him and took up for him.
So, for a brief period, Saul was a regular member of the Jerusalem church. Was it out of respect for Stephen that he attempted
soon to argue with the Hellenists? The results were the same.
They tried to kill him. But the brethren discovered the plot in
time, took Saul down to Caesarea, and put him on the boat for
Tarsus.

This is one of the most difficult passages in Acts to reconcile
with what Paul tells about himself in his letters. In Galatians
1:16-17, he says that following his conversion, "I did not confer

with flesh and blood, nor did I go up to Jerusalem to those who were apostles before me, but I went away into Arabia; and again I returned to Damascus." In II Corinthians 11:32, he states that it was the governor under King Aretas (an Arabian ruler) who was watching the gates of Damascus in order to seize him. Three years later he did go to Jerusalem, but apparently spent his time in private conferences with Peter and James, for "I was still not known by sight to the churches of Christ in Judea" (see Galatians 1:18-24).

Our information is entirely too sketchy for us to say that these differences can or cannot be reconciled. Their importance has been overemphasized. All sources agree: (1) that Saul was converted on the road to Damascus; (2) that he preached in Damascus; (3) that afterward he was in contact with the church at Jerusalem; (4) that the contact was brief.

Peter Opens the Door to Gentiles (9:31—11:18)

A Peaceful Era for the Church (9:31)

With the leading persecutor converted, the Church now enjoyed a period of peaceful growth. This summary (compare 2:43-47; 4:32-35; 5:12-16; 6:7) is notable for three things: (1) here the word "church" is used, not for one local congregation, but for the entire body of all congregations; (2) only here is the Church in Galilee mentioned; it must have been strong and important, including many of the nameless people whom Jesus himself had taught and healed, even though Luke did not choose to tell us more about it; (3) here it is abundantly clear that the Holy Spirit rests upon the whole Church, not just a few exceptional individuals.

Peter at Lydda and Joppa (9:32-43)

Luke now tells some specific stories from this brief, peaceful era. Once again Peter leaves his post at Jerusalem to follow up and confirm the work of Philip. The cities that he visits—Lydda, Joppa, and Caesarea—had all been evangelized by Philip (see 8:40). This explains why Peter found "saints" there. If "the Way" was a name given the Church by its enemies (see the comment on 9:1-9), "saints" was what the believers liked to call themselves (see 9:13, 32, 41). It means "holy ones" or "ones set apart." In modern times it is often restricted to persons of exceptional piety, but in the New Testament it applies to all the members of the Church.

At Lydda, Peter healed a bedridden man named Aeneas. And at Joppa, he raised Dorcas from the dead. Miracles of healing have been frequent thus far in Acts, but a restoration of the dead to life is something new. The raising of Dorcas is similar to the raising of the widow's son by Elijah (I Kings 17:17-24); the very similar story told of Elisha (II Kings 4:32-37); the raising of the son of the widow of Nain (Luke 7:11-17); and the raising of Jairus' daughter (Luke 8:40-56). In all these cases, the raising occurred quickly, before burial. It was more a revival of breath and consciousness than resurrection from the tomb. In all these cases, victory over death was temporary; these people later died. They are extraordinary healings; but they are not comparable to the resurrection of Jesus, who "being raised from the dead will never die again" (Romans 6:9).

The raising of Dorcas opened the door for a fruitful ministry in Joppa, which was an important seaport town. Peter resolved to stay there, and took lodging with one Simon, a tanner. This was unusual, since tanning was regarded as an unclean profession by strict Jews.

Peter Goes to Cornelius (10:1-33)

By far the most important event on Peter's missionary journey was the conversion of Cornelius. Cornelius was a Roman army officer, stationed in Caesarea. This city had been rebuilt by Herod and named in honor of Caesar Augustus. It was the chief port of Palestine and the official Roman capital of the provinces of Judea and Samaria. There the Roman governor, or procurator, had his headquarters. He was in Jerusalem, usually, only during the feasts. The Italian Cohort, made up largely of freedmen, was probably a special detachment of troops, to be used by the governor to put down disorders that might arise among the Jews.

Cornelius, weary of Roman paganism, had been attracted by Judaism. Verse 2 describes him as an ideal "God-fearer." In a vision, he was directed to send to Joppa for Peter.

The next day, as Cornelius' messengers were approaching, Peter, in his turn, had a vision. The form in which Peter's vision came was very natural under the circumstances. The great sheet, or sail, may have been suggested to him by the sails on boats in the harbor. And the animals, to be eaten, may have been suggested by the fact that it was noon and he was hungry. But the essential message of the vision was contrary to all his past conditioning and training. The animals in the sheet were unclean; that is, they were animals which the Law of Moses forbade Jews to eat (Lev. 11). The voice in his vision commanded: "Rise, Peter; kill and eat." Peter refused on the all-too-human grounds: "No Lord; for I have never . . ." It is equally possible today to refuse to obey the clear command of God simply because we have never done the thing we now see to be his will. The voice replied: "What God has cleansed, you must not call common." Peter did not yet understand Jesus' words about what truly defiles a man (Mark 7:18-19). Three times the command came. And three times Peter refused.

Just at this moment, when Peter was greatly perplexed, he heard men below calling his name, asking if he were staying there. The Spirit assured him that this was no accident: the vision and the human messengers were connected; he must go with them. What hesitations did he have to overcome to invite them in for the night? What misgivings did he have as he journeyed with them for two days on the road to Caesarea? As a precaution, he took six brethren from Joppa as witnesses (11:12).

Quite a reception awaited Peter and his party at Caesarea. Cornelius had assembled his kinsmen and friends. When Peter entered, Cornelius attempted to worship him, but Peter prevented him. Upon seeing the large crowd of Gentiles, Peter's prejudice rose to his throat, and he felt compelled to say that he was present only by the direct revelation of God. He had come to understand at least that the animals in his vision signified *men* (vs. 28). Cornelius recounted the vision which led him to send for Peter. He concluded: "Now therefore we are all here present in the sight of God, to hear all that you have been commanded by the Lord." Any preacher would give the half of his kingdom to be so addressed by his congregation.

The Sermon in Cornelius' House (10:34-43)

Moved by Cornelius' evident sincerity, Peter preaches an eloquent sermon. In some ways this is the most important of all the examples of the apostolic preaching in Acts. After confessing that he himself is learning much from this experience about the impartiality of God, Peter states the essential facts about Jesus as follows: (1) John preached and baptized; (2) God anointed

Jesus of Nazareth with the Holy Spirit and with power; (3) Jesus went about Galilee, doing good, healing, casting out demons; (4) he went to Jerusalem; (5) they crucified him; (6) God raised him on the third day; (7) the chosen disciples saw him and ate with him; (8) he commanded them to preach and witness to him. Anyone who is reasonably familiar with the Gospel of Mark will immediately recognize that this is Mark's outline. Our oldest Gospel may well be described as an expansion of Peter's sermon.

Peter not only tells the straightforward story of Jesus, but he indicates something of its theological significance. Jesus is: (1) Lord of all; (2) the one ordained by God to be the judge of all the living and the dead; (3) the fulfillment of all the prophecies; (4) the one through whose name forgiveness may be received by everyone. Notice the universal appeal of this sermon, with the repeated "all" and the final inclusive "every one."

The Witness of the Spirit (10:44-48)

Peter planned to say more (see 11:15), but there was a glorious interruption. The Holy Spirit "fell on" all who heard (compare with 8:16). Verse 46 leaves no doubt that the outward form of this "falling" of the Holy Spirit was speaking in tongues. This is the second of the three exceptional cases where water-baptism and Spirit-baptism are separated in Acts (see the comment on 8:14-25). But this time the Spirit-baptism *precedes* the water-baptism. The Spirit blows where he wills (see John 3:8), and will not be tied to any outward form. Not by human manipulation, but of his own sovereign will, he fell upon the Gentiles of Caesarea.

If this had not happened, we cannot be sure Peter would have offered to receive them into the Church. To his mind, the Church was still a sect within Judaism. And even though God had sent Cornelius a vision, even though Cornelius' devotion was most acceptable to God, still Cornelius was not a Jew. Nor were his friends. All these hesitations, however, vanished when the Spirit came. The logic of the situation became perfectly clear: the Spirit had already included these men in the Church; could a human being, then, refuse them the usual rite of initiation? Of course not! Peter therefore commanded them to be baptized. And he stayed for some days to see that this new church was well established.

Peter Defends His Actions (11:1-18)

The reception of Gentiles into the Church cut across deep-seated traditions and prejudices. When Peter reached Jerusalem, he faced bitter questioners. Here for the first time we read of "the circumcision party." These earnest Jewish believers had set up an artificial restriction in the Church. The Church must be "for Jews only." Even so, this was less extreme than many a modern restriction, for example, the racial bar. In the modern concept, there is no way a man can change his race. To the circumcision party, the restriction was not a matter of race but of circumcision. A Gentile who wished to become a Jew had only to be circumcised. Once that was done, he could be admitted to the Church. The part of Peter's conduct that was particularly offensive to these men was his staying and eating with uncircumcised Gentiles. It is always at this point that prejudiced people are most deeply disturbed.

Peter's defense consisted of a simple retelling of just what had happened. He had his six witnesses with him to vouch for the truth of what he said (vs. 12). He justified baptizing the Gentiles by quoting Jesus' promise of Spirit-baptism (vs. 16; compare 1:5). He ended with an unanswerable question: "Who was I that I could withstand God?"

His opponents were silenced. For the time being the argument was settled, although it was to break out again (see 15:1). The Early Church was prepared to accept the verdict of the Spirit. If the Spirit had marked these men out as belonging to Christ, then to refuse to acknowledge them as brothers in the Church, no matter how strong tradition and prejudice might be, was to withstand God. The lesson for our own day is obvious.

The Church at Antioch (11:19-30)

The Church Is Founded (11:19-21)

The persecution that arose over Stephen had resulted in Philip's evangelistic labors (8:4-40), Saul's conversion (9:1-30), and Peter's missionary work (9:31—11:18). One further result remains to be noted: the foundation of the church at Antioch.

Antioch was the third city of the Roman world. Only Rome and Alexandria were larger. It had been the capital of the great Seleucid Empire, which controlled the Near East from the death of Alex-

ander until the coming of the Romans. As in all the major cities
of the Roman Empire, there was a Jewish community in Antioch.
The refugees from Jerusalem preached to them that Jesus was
Lord. But some of the refugees, men from Cyprus and Cyrene
who had lived among Gentiles all their lives, went further; they
preached to the Greeks also. The word "Greeks," or as some
manuscripts give it, "Hellenists," must surely refer here to Gentiles, not to Hellenist Jews. The Gentiles of Antioch received the
gospel enthusiastically, and in great numbers.

The Ministry of Barnabas and Saul (11:22-26)

Each new development seems to have caused concern to the
conservative church in Jerusalem. Barnabas was dispatched to
investigate. When he examined the situation he found it to be a
great demonstration, not of human rashness, but of God's grace.
So he gladly joined in the work. In effect, he became the pastor of
the church there. His qualifications for the task were excellent:
(1) a good man; (2) full of the Holy Spirit; (3) full of faith.
Under his ministry, the church grew too large for one pastor. So
Barnabas went to Tarsus and brought back Saul as his associate.
For a year they had a fruitful ministry together.

Jewish critics had called the believers "the Way" in derision.
Now their heathen neighbors taunted them with the name "Christians," which means "partisans or followers of Christ." This is the
name that stuck. It is the glory of the Church that its members
are known the world over, to this day, as "followers of Christ." It
is also a deep shame that "for Christians only" is the slogan of
anti-Semitism, and that various fascist movements vaunt themselves as "Christian." It is not without significance that the church
which first dropped all artificial restrictions and admitted both
Jews and Gentiles without distinction was the church which
earned this glorious name. Can it be rightfully used by churches
which after 1900 years still lag behind Antioch in this respect?

Relief Sent to Judea (11:27-30)

The church at Antioch further demonstrated genuine Christianity by sending famine relief to the brethren in Judea—the very
ones who had been most critical of them.

Here we meet for the first time in Acts the Christian prophets.
It was a common belief among the Jews that the ancient order of
prophets had come to an end in the days of Ezra. Prophecy would

be restored only in the last days. This, the Church claimed, is precisely what had happened at Pentecost (see 2:17-21). In the outpouring of the Spirit, the office of prophet had been restored. So we meet Christian prophets in many places in the New Testament (Acts 13:1; 15:32; 19:6; 21:9-11; Rom. 12:6; I Cor. 12-14; Eph. 2:20; 3:5; 4:11; Rev. 22:9). Often the New Testament prophets are explained simply as eloquent preachers. But they were a distinct order, specially endowed by the Spirit. And, like the Old Testament prophets, though they were concerned primarily to declare the present will of God, they had the gift of predicting future events. Here Agabus predicts a great famine.

In this passage we meet the first definite reference in Acts to contemporary Roman history: "the days of Claudius." Not since Luke 3:1 has the reigning Caesar been named. These two references show that the ministry of Jesus and the early history of the Church down to the church at Antioch all took place between A.D. 27 (the fifteenth year of Tiberius) and about A.D. 46 (Claudius reigned from A.D. 41-54). It is impossible to date the individual events more precisely.

Here also, the primitive "communism" of the Church took a new form. The younger churches would share with the mother church at Jerusalem. Famine would strike Jerusalem with particular severity, since the city could not support its normal population for long without food from the outside. In this offering, the characteristic principle of Christian stewardship was already at work. No tax or assessment was imposed; everyone gave "according to his ability" (compare I Cor. 16:2).

The offering was entrusted to Saul and Barnabas for delivery. Notice that the officers of the church at Jerusalem were by now called "elders." Had there been further organizational development, since the Apostles were now engaged more and more outside Jerusalem? This offering would surely have been delivered to "the seven" if they were still in charge of the daily distribution (see the comment on 6:2-6). Had the elders succeeded the seven, or had the seven themselves been elders? There is much we do not know about the organization of the Early Church.

The Persecution Under Herod (12:1-23)

James Is Killed; Peter Imprisoned (12:1-5)

"Herod the king," in this passage, is Herod Agrippa I. From the time Rome seized Palestine in 63 B.C. until about A.D. 100, the Romans constantly relied upon one family of Idumean (Edomite) rulers to help them maintain order among the Jews. This was the family of the Herods.

Like all the other Herods, Agrippa remained completely loyal to Rome. But unlike all the others, he won the affection of the Jews. His grandmother had been a princess of the old Maccabean line, and so was his wife. The Jewish people hailed him as a brother and disregarded the hated Idumean lineage he had through his grandfather. His popularity was enhanced because at great political risk he had resisted the plan of Caligula to set up a statue of himself in the Temple.

It was in an effort to enhance his popularity still further that he ordered the execution of James, one of the original Apostles. It is evident that the Church had never regained the favor with the masses which was lost at the death of Stephen. Doubtless reports that the Jewish Christians were eating and worshiping with Gentiles added to their unpopularity. The Jewish populace were delighted to see their king persecute "the Way."

Thus encouraged, Agrippa had Peter arrested. As had been the case when Peter's Master was arrested, the Feast of Unleavened Bread was at hand. Not wishing to interrupt the feast with an execution, Agrippa had Peter held in prison under strong guard. In the meantime, the Christians were in earnest prayer. Their very existence was threatened, for the legal safeguards of the Sanhedrin, the level thinking of men like Gamaliel, were no protection against Herod the king. He could have them all killed. And it seemed he would, if it pleased the Jews.

Peter's Miraculous Escape (12:6-17)

The night before he was to be brought out for execution, Peter was miraculously delivered from prison. In spite of Herod's elaborate precautions, an angel entered his cell and delivered him. (For a similar story and a discussion of angels, see the comment on 5:17-26.) Peter thought he was seeing a vision until he found himself alone in the street.

He went immediately to the house of Mary, the mother of John Mark. This may or may not have been the location of the traditional "upper room." But it was evidently a common meeting place for the Christians of Jerusalem. A prayer meeting was in progress. When Rhoda reported that Peter was outside, they would not believe her. How often we pray earnestly, but do not really expect an answer to our prayers! How often when the answer comes we refuse to recognize it!

Peter made a brief report of his deliverance and asked them to tell this "to James and to the brethren." James the brother of John had been beheaded. This is the first mention in Acts of another James, who emerges from this point on as the real head of the church at Jerusalem. According to Galatians 1:19 this James was the brother of Jesus himself. He had seen the Risen Lord (see I Cor. 15:7). As a result he had joined the little waiting band in the Upper Room (see Acts 1:14). From that time his influence had been increasing. Peter wisely left the city, following his escape from prison, and the leadership of the Jerusalem church passed to James.

The Death of the Persecutor (12:18-23)

Enraged over Peter's escape, Herod had the sentries executed. It is a hard fact that the innocent sometimes suffer from the crimes of the wicked.

Herod returned to his capital at Caesarea. There he met a sensational end. Josephus, the Jewish historian, gives a slightly different account, but agrees with Acts that he was suddenly stricken as the people called him a god. To be eaten by worms was considered the most disgraceful of all deaths.

THE WITNESS TO THE END OF THE EARTH
Acts 12:24—28:31

The Mission to Galatia (12:24—14:28)

Continued Growth (12:24)

We have noted previously how Luke punctuates his book with general summaries that are reports on the state of the Church. It is clear that most of these summaries are introductions rather than conclusions (see 2:43-47; 4:32-35; 5:12-16; 6:7; 9:31).

The summary in 12:24 may be the exception, forming the conclusion to the story of Herod. Certainly it presents a vivid contrast: the tyrant is eaten by worms and dies; but the word of God
which he sought to suppress continues to grow and multiply.
However, it forms an equally admirable introduction to the whole
story of Paul's missionary labors. What were these labors but a
growing and multiplying of the word of God?

Mark Enlists in the Mission (12:25)

Verse 25 presents many difficulties. It is evidently the conclusion of the story found in 11:27-30. The impression is given that
Saul and Barnabas arrived in Jerusalem before Peter's arrest (see
11:30); that they were there during all the events of chapter 12;
and that after Herod's death they returned to Antioch. This can
hardly be so. All the facts we can gather point to A.D. 44 as the
year of Herod's death and A.D. 46 as the year of the famine. This
means that, although the prediction of Agabus and the raising of
the relief fund may have preceded the events of chapter 12, the
actual mission of Barnabas and Saul did not take place until two
years after the death of Herod. In other words, the whole Herod
story belongs, chronologically, between 11:29 and 11:30, rather
than between 11:30 and 12:25.

Related to this confusion of time is a confusion of the text.
The best manuscripts say in 12:25 that Saul and Barnabas returned *to* Jerusalem. Surely they did go *to* Jerusalem following
Herod's death. But Mark did not accompany them *to* Jerusalem;
they brought him back *from* Jerusalem.

In spite of the confusion of our records, the facts are clear
enough. A year or two after Herod's death, Saul and Barnabas
carried the relief money to the churches of Judea and then returned to Antioch, bringing with them John Mark. Mark was a
cousin of Barnabas (Col. 4:10).

Saul and Barnabas Commissioned (13:1-3)

The church at Antioch had pioneered in breaking down the
barrier between Jew and Gentile. It had pioneered in sending
out the first relief expedition in Christian history. Now it takes
the lead in launching the foreign missionary enterprise. Up to
this point, the Church had spread chiefly through refugees, flee-
ing persecution. But at Antioch men were sent out for the set
purpose of proclaiming the gospel where it had not been heard.

The officers of the church at Antioch were prophets and teachers. Elected and appointed officers seem to have been the rule in the church at Jerusalem: the Twelve (see 1:15-26), the seven (see 6:1-6), and the elders (see 11:30). But in the Early Church we also find leaders who were neither elected nor appointed, but who attained their office in the Church by a special gift of the Spirit. They are often called *charismatic* leaders, which means "gifted" leaders. Lists of such offices are found in Romans 12: 6-8; I Corinthians 12:28; and Ephesians 4:11. Prophets and teachers were genuine charismatics, men with special spiritual gifts. (See the comment on 11:27-30 for further discussion on the prophets.)

The Spirit had bestowed his gifts on a mixed group of men at Antioch. Barnabas was a devout Jew, a native of Cyprus. Symeon was nicknamed "the Black," which may indicate that he was a Negro; it is not impossible to identify him with the Simon who bore Jesus' cross (Luke 23:26). Lucius was from Cyrene in North Africa. There has been some attempt to identify him with Luke, the author of Acts, but this is unlikely. Manaen had been a boyhood companion of Herod the Tetrarch. Saul had been the most zealous of Pharisees, the persecutor of the Church.

As they prayed and fasted together, these charismatic leaders received a revelation of the Spirit. Barnabas and Saul were to be set apart for a special work and sent away from Antioch. These were their two most able leaders. How natural it would have been for them to select men whom the home church could more easily spare! But the Spirit had spoken, and they obeyed without question. After further fasting and prayer, they laid their hands on them (compare 6:6) and sent them off.

Preaching in Cyprus (13:4-12)

The first missionaries began their travels in a world that seemed providentially prepared for such work. Rome ruled. Men could travel, without passports and without the dangers of war, anywhere in the empire. Except in winter, sea travel was good: pirates had been swept from the Mediterranean; good harbors were maintained; flourishing trade made boats readily available for almost any destination. Land travel was equally good on the famous network of Roman roads. Messengers often covered twenty-five miles a day on foot, and the Emperor Tiberius once traveled two hundred miles in twenty-four hours on a relay of fast horses.

It has been said that in the first century one could travel in Mediterranean lands with less "red tape" and more security than has ever been possible since.

Saul and Barnabas took a boat from Seleucia, which was the seaport for Antioch, and sailed to the island of Cyprus, which was Barnabas' home. They began their work in the city of Salamis, the chief commercial center of the island. Following the usual policy (see 9:20), they preached first to the Jews in their synagogues. John Mark had come with them and assisted them in this work.

From Salamis, they crossed the island to Paphos, the capital city. Here was the residence of Sergius Paulus, the Roman proconsul who governed the island in the name of the Roman Senate. Luke, as usual, is scrupulously accurate in the title given this Roman official. The proconsul had an inquiring mind, and when he learned of the new teachers, he sent to hear them. A local Jewish magician named Bar-Jesus (compare the magician in 8:9-24) saw his influence and profits threatened, and attempted to withstand the missionaries. Saul, who had deferred to Barnabas up to this point, received a sudden infilling of spiritual power. He administered a severe rebuke and the magician was struck with temporary blindness. The proconsul was amazed and believed. There is some question whether this means that he actually became a convert.

It is in connection with this incident that Luke begins to call his hero Paul. Saul was his Jewish name. As a member of the tribe of Benjamin (Phil. 3:5) he had been named for Israel's first king, the most illustrious of all Benjaminites (I Sam. 10:20-24). But as a Roman citizen (22:25-29) the Apostle also bore the good Latin name Paulus, or Paul. It is an interesting coincidence that this is the same name borne by the proconsul.

The Expedition Enters Galatia (13:13-15)

After the incident at Paphos, Paul definitely took the lead. The expedition is now called "Paul and his company." By boat they crossed to the mainland and journeyed inland to Perga, the principal city of the small province of Pamphylia. At that point, John Mark deserted the expedition and returned to Jerusalem. It has been guessed that he disliked seeing his cousin Barnabas replaced by Paul as the leader, or that he disapproved of the conversion of Gentiles, or that he was simply homesick. Whatever his reason may have been, Paul felt that it was insufficient (see 15:38).

The remaining members of the party soon left the lowlands of Pamphylia, and climbing the Taurus Mountains reached a high plateau some thirty-six hundred feet above sea level. They had entered the extensive Roman province of Galatia. On the basis of Galatians 4:13 it has been suggested that Paul sought this high country because his health suffered in the lowlands.

Their first stop in Galatia was a city called Pisidian Antioch. It was not actually in the ancient kingdom of Pisidia but was near its border. This Antioch was a Roman colony, settled by retired soldiers. It is not to be confused with Antioch in Syria, the great city from which the missionaries had come. As was customary, the visitors to the synagogue were given an opportunity to speak, if they desired.

The Sermon at Pisidian Antioch (13:16-43)

Paul stood and gestured with his hand for silence. The sermon which follows is the longest sample we have of his preaching. It closely resembles the sermons of Peter, and yet there are interesting differences.

In addressing his audience (vss. 16, 26) Paul includes the two classes of his hearers—the Jews and the God-fearing Gentiles who were present in the synagogue. He reviews the history of Israel from the Exodus down to David. As a loyal Benjaminite he does not neglect to mention Saul, for whom he was named (vs. 21).

He jumps from David to David's descendant, Jesus. The essential facts of Jesus' life are related: the ministry of John, the trial before Pilate, the crucifixion, the burial, the resurrection. All these things are the fulfillment of Scripture, Paul declares, quoting from Psalm 2, Isaiah 55, and Psalm 16. His argument from Psalm 16 is exactly that of Peter (compare 13:35-37 with 2:25-31).

It is in the conclusion (vss. 38-41) that Paul's own distinctive understanding of the gospel begins to show itself. Unlike Peter, Paul had been a Pharisee. As a Pharisee, the heart of his religion had been the effort to keep the Law of Moses down to its minutest details. Every failure to do so had added to the weight of his sin, sin for which he tried to atone by an even more rigorous keeping of the Law. The Law had thus been the intolerable burden of his life. In Christ he had found forgiveness for his sin and freedom from the Law. The word "freed" in verse 39 is "justified," which Paul so often uses in his letters. It is the gospel of release for the individual here and now which he proclaims. It even overshadows, in this sermon, the exaltation of Christ to God's right hand and the hope of his coming again—the characteristic closing notes of the apostolic preaching. He ends with a solemn warning against unbelief.

Those who heard Paul were deeply stirred. He was asked to preach again the following Sabbath. Many, both Jews and Gentile proselytes, became followers of Paul and Barnabas and received further instruction.

"We Turn to the Gentiles" (13:44-52)

The next Sabbath the Jews of Pisidian Antioch were greeted by an unusual sight. Their synagogue was packed; the crowd overflowed into the street; almost the whole city was there. For years it had been their ambition to exalt the God of their fathers that his name might be feared to the ends of the earth. But now that it had happened, now that the synagogue had attracted the attention of the whole city, they were angry. This unexpected success had come, not to the faithful few who had supported the synagogue Sabbath after Sabbath, but to strangers.

Mad with jealousy, the Jews turned against Paul and Barnabas. They interrupted the sermon. They contradicted Paul's interpretation of the Scriptures. They called him names. Finally, Paul and Barnabas came to a momentous decision: since the Jews had rejected the gospel, the missionaries would turn to the Gentiles. They claimed God's command to his Servant in Isaiah 49:6 as authority for this. Behind such a use of Scripture lies the unspoken understanding that the Servant's task, which Israel had failed to perform, and which Jesus had adopted as his pattern, was now the responsibility of the Church.

There is no doubt that in Luke's understanding the turn to the Gentiles in this passage was a decisive moment in the development of the Church. Up to this point the mission of the Church had been directed to the Jewish synagogue. Gentiles had been accepted into the Church, but they had come by way of the synagogue. The Ethiopian eunuch, Cornelius, the Greeks at Antioch —all these had been God-fearing Gentiles who worshiped in the synagogue and studied the Scriptures long before they heard the gospel. But in the crowd at Pisidian Antioch that day were Gentiles who had never been in a synagogue before. And they were just as receptive to the gospel as the Jews were hostile. Paul and Barnabas resolved to turn to these people and to work with them outside the synagogue, if necessary.

The announcement of this change of policy had a double effect. (1) Among the Gentiles, there was great gladness. Many were converted; some were not. Luke sees God's electing grace at work here (vs. 48). The converts rapidly spread the gospel throughout Phrygia, which was the region about Antioch. (2) Among the Jews, there was bitter hostility. It is interesting that some of the Gentiles who had been adherents to Judaism before Paul came supported the Jews. Members of the upper social strata —"devout women of high standing and the leading men of the city"—had been God-fearers. They seem to have resented, as did the Jews, the free offer of the gospel to the masses. Using these powerful allies, the Jews had Paul and Barnabas run out of town.

The mission to Pisidian Antioch was over. The missionaries, with typical Eastern symbolism, shook the dust of Antioch from their feet (compare Luke 9:5; 10:10-11). The disciples whom they left behind were disorganized, but they possessed the unmistakable mark of the Church: they were filled with joy and with the Holy Spirit. Thus it was clear that divine approval rested upon the turning to the Gentiles.

Forced to Leave Iconium (14:1-7)

The missionaries followed the great royal highway south and east to Iconium. Here again they began their work in the synagogue. They met with initial success. But once again the Jews, with Gentile allies, turned against them. In spite of the opposition, the work went on; the Spirit bore witness to their preaching by signs and wonders. Finally the tension in the synagogue spread until the whole city was divided. The Jews persuaded the magistrates that the missionaries were a threat to peace. Learning that they were about to be attacked and stoned, Paul and Barnabas fled farther to the south, into the ancient kingdom of Lycaonia, now also a part of the Roman province of Galatia.

Worshiped at Lystra (14:8-20)

The next city on their route was Lystra. Although there were some Jews at Lystra (see 16:1), no mention is made of a synagogue there. The story that is told represents a contact between the Christian faith and the ancient paganism that still flourished, particularly in remote cities such as Lystra.

One day when the city was crowded, perhaps for a pagan festival, Paul healed a man who had been a cripple from his birth (compare the story about Peter in 3:1-10). The Apostles required faith in those whom they were to heal (vs. 9), just as Jesus did (compare Luke 8:48; 18:42). When the man sprang up and walked, the crowds were stirred. They put a typical pagan interpretation on what they had seen: the gods had visited them in human form. They were sure that Barnabas, who must have been a large, heavily bearded man, was Zeus (or Jupiter), the king of the gods. They identified Paul, who must have been smaller and quick in his movements, and who apparently was the spokesman, as Hermes (or Mercury). Word was sent to the local priest of Zeus, who brought oxen and garlands to the gates and prepared to offer a sacrifice to Paul and Barnabas.

While all this was going on, the missionaries were innocently watching the excitement, unable to understand the ancient Lycaonian language which people still spoke in this remote district. When the priest arrived with the oxen, they finally realized what was happening. In a typical Eastern gesture, they tore their garments (compare Mark 14:63), and rushed out among the multitude, crying, "We also are men, of like nature with you."

There follows a brief example of an apostolic sermon, as preached to a pagan crowd such as this one. There could be no appeal here to the Old Testament Scriptures. The theme is rather the living God, who is contrasted with "these vain things." This living God, Paul declares, is the Creator, the Maker of all things. In the past he allowed the nations to walk in their own ways. Yet even in the past, men should have recognized him by his goodness to them. Clearly the sermon is leading up to the point: "But now, this living God has made himself known in Jesus." Why Luke does not record the rest of the sermon here, we cannot say; but the sermon to the pagans at Athens (see 17: 22-31) shows how it must have ended.

Not long after this colorful incident, the mission to Lystra came to an abrupt end. The Jews from Antioch and Iconium pursued the missionaries there, stirred up a mob, stoned Paul, and dragged him out of the city, supposing that he was dead. Paul now tasted what once had happened to Stephen. Stephen's stoning, however, may have been the regular Jewish method of execution (see comment on 7:54—8:3). In Paul's case, he was doubtless pelted with small stones such as a mob could snatch up. He was stunned, but not dead. When he came to, he saw the anxious faces of his converts in Lystra, gathered about him in prayer and sympathy. He was able to get up and to be helped into the city. By the next day he was strong enough to go on with Barnabas to Derbe.

The Return to Antioch (14:21-28)

Only the briefest record is given of the mission to Derbe. Apparently it was successful and uneventful. At Derbe, Paul and Barnabas were on the southeastern border of the Roman province of Galatia. A good road lay ahead of them to Tarsus and on around to Antioch, their home base. But they were concerned about the little groups of believers from whom they had had to flee. Therefore, in the face of great danger they returned to Lystra, then to Iconium, then to Antioch. Either because new magistrates were now in office, or because they worked in secret, they escaped persecution. They strengthened the little churches, reassured them, and ordained elders (see 11:30). The Greek of verse 23 seems to say that Paul and Barnabas elected the elders for the churches. Whether the churches themselves voted is not clear. At any rate, charismatic leaders alone were not sufficient to maintain the order of the Church in times of persecution. In each church, before departing, a solemn service of prayer and fasting was held, committing the new believers to Christ's care.

From Pisidian Antioch they retraced their route to Perga. This time Paul's health permitted him to preach there. From Attalia, Perga's seaport, they sailed back to Syrian Antioch. There they made a full report to the whole church. The wording is interesting: not what they had done, but all that God had done with them. They did not dwell on their sufferings but on their opportunities. They attached the highest significance to the decision at Pisidian Antioch; there God had opened a door of faith to the Gentiles. After the report was made, the missionaries resumed their ministry in the church at Antioch.

The Debate Over Circumcision (15:1-35)

The Issue (15:1-5)

The success of the Gentile mission brought to the surface a deep, underlying theological problem which had to be faced sooner or later. What was the real relationship of Christianity to Judaism? At the first, without thinking it through, the Jerusalem Christians had assumed that they were a sect within Judaism. They all bore on their bodies the Jewish mark of circumcision; they all knew the Jewish Scriptures; they all worshiped at the Temple. It is true that they were a pure Israel within a corrupt Israel, yet they were Israel all the same. But as the Church spread, under the guidance of the Spirit, more and more men came into the New Israel who had not been a part of the Old. Proselytes were acceptable, of course, since they had been officially members of Israel. The God-fearing Gentiles were questionable, but at least they knew the Scriptures and worshiped in the synagogue. But could a rank pagan come into the Church, having never been remotely connected with Israel before? If this were permitted, then Christianity would be a new religion and not a part of Judaism at all!

Once before, the conservatives in the church at Jerusalem had sought to stop this dangerous drift (see 11:1-18). They had been temporarily silenced by Peter, but they continued to have misgivings, particularly about the brash young church at Antioch. When rumors of what had happened in Galatia arrived, they determined to make a resolute stand. Their strongest support came from the converted Pharisees (vs. 5).

These conservatives worked out their platform carefully. They decided to center their argument on the issue of salvation itself. How is a man to be saved in the day of final judgment? The answer of the Pharisees was sure and clear: by keeping the Law of Moses. We should not marvel that men could become Christians, accept Jesus as the Messiah, and still believe in salvation by works of the Law. There is a Pharisee deep in every man; and the working religion of a multitude of modern Christians is legalism.

Now circumcision was a part of the Law of Moses. Therefore, the Pharisee-Christians reasoned, no man can be saved who has not been circumcised. Whether a man has kept the other laws may be a matter of opinion, but circumcision is a tangible fact. Let all the new converts from the Gentiles be circumcised and undertake to keep the Law of Moses. This would settle the difficulty and Christianity would remain a sect within Israel.

This doctrine was carried straight to Antioch. Paul and Barnabas disagreed strongly. The contention destroyed the peace of the Church. So Paul and Barnabas and others were appointed to go up to Jerusalem to the Apostles and the elders, to find some way to settle the issue. On their way they reported to the churches of Phoenicia and Samaria the success of the Gentile mission and received widespread support for what they had done. When they reached Jerusalem, they made a complete report to the Jerusalem church. The issue was soon drawn. The circumcision-Pharisee party rose up and said that they must go back to those people, circumcise them, and charge them to keep the Law of Moses.

Peter's Testimony (15:6-11)

A special meeting was held to consider the matter. It was not a general council of the whole Church, for it appears that only Antioch and Jerusalem were represented. Yet its decisions were apparently considered binding for all Christians. Very naturally, the original Apostles were considered to have a unique authority.

Luke tells us that there was much debate, but with typical selectivity he gives us the gist of three speeches. Peter spoke first. The great weight of his authority was cast on the side of Antioch. He appeals to his experience with Cornelius and argues as before that the gift of the Spirit decides the matter. To take the Pharisee position, he says, is to tempt God. He calls the Law a yoke which the Jews had never been able to bear. Why put it on the neck of new converts? He comes to the heart of the issue in his conclusion: salvation is through the grace of the Lord Jesus, not through keeping the Law. Jew and Gentile alike will be saved through grace.

Paul and Barnabas' Testimony (15:12)

Paul and Barnabas next took the floor. Their main argument rested on the signs and wonders which God had done through them on the Gentile mission. Signs and wonders are evidences of the Spirit's working. The Spirit had witnessed to their work in Galatia as clearly as to Peter's work in Caesarea.

James' Judgment (15:13-21)

James was now head of the church at Jerusalem (see 12:17).
He assumed the responsibility of summing up the debate and giv-
ing "the sense of the meeting." He seems to ignore Paul and
Barnabas. He gives more weight to the words of Symeon (Peter).
But most weight goes to the words of the prophets. He quotes
Amos 9:11-12 from a text quite different from the Hebrew text
we now have. The principle which James regards as established
is that God has always purposed the conversion of the Gentiles.
Into the vital issue of whether salvation is by law or by grace,
he does not enter.

He proposes a practical compromise. Circumcision will not be
required of the Gentile converts. But they will be asked to abstain
from those features of Gentile life which are particularly abhor-
rent to Jews: the eating of meat offered to idols, unchastity, eating meat that has been "strangled" (not properly bled), and
eating blood. If the Gentile Christians would do this much, it
would make it far easier for Jewish Christians to associate with
them. The argument in verse 21 is hard to follow, but clearly
it is intended to make it easier for the Pharisee party to accept
this compromise. The Law of Moses is not discredited. Anyone,
said James, can hear it on any Sabbath in any city.

The Jerusalem Decree (15:22-35)

The compromise of James won the day. Since Antioch had
sent a delegation to Jerusalem, Jerusalem decided to return the
courtesy and send a delegation to Antioch. Judas, called Barsabbas, may have been a brother of Joseph called Barsabbas (see
Acts 1:23), though no early tradition connects them. Silas is the
same as Silvanus (see I Thess. 1:1). These two were sent, bearing
an official letter from the Jerusalem church to all the Gentile
Christians in Antioch and its surrounding province of Syria and
Cilicia.

The letter clearly states that the circumcision party did not
speak officially for the Jerusalem church. It shows that Paul and
Barnabas were considered Christians in good standing. The
heart of the letter (vss. 28-29) contains the four restrictions suggested by James, though in a different order. The Jerusalem
church adds its judgment that this decision is inspired by the
Holy Spirit himself.

The letter was duly delivered to the congregation at Antioch, who rejoiced over it. Judas and Silas had the spiritual gift of prophecy and spent some time in Antioch making prophetic utterances and strengthening the brethren. They returned finally to Jerusalem, and Paul and Barnabas continued their ministry in Antioch.

There is a minor difficulty in the story. Soon Silas was to leave Antioch with Paul on his next journey (see 15:40). Early scribes saw this problem and inserted verse 34: "But it seemed good to Silas to remain there" (margin).

The Problem of Galatians

Thus far we have considered Luke's record of the debate over circumcision just as it stands. It contains some puzzles, to be sure. The actual decree seems to be an answer to the question: What is necessary before Jewish Christians and Gentile Christians may eat together? It ignores the basic question which started the dispute: Is circumcision necessary for salvation? Even so, it would not occur to us to question Luke's record if we did not have the Letter to the Galatians.

In the Letter to the Galatians, we meet the same two issues: the relation of circumcision to salvation and the table fellowship of Jewish and Gentile Christians. Apparently neither issue has been settled at all. Men from the circumcision party have turned Paul's Galatian churches against Paul and his teaching and have persuaded many that they must be circumcised. Men sent from James have broken up the table fellowship that existed at Antioch, carrying Peter and even Barnabas with them. Paul, on the other hand, will accept no such compromise as recorded in Acts 15. No part of the Law is binding on Christians save the inner law of love.

To make matters more complicated, Paul records in Galatians 2:1-10 a conference at Jerusalem. It is hard to believe it is not the same conference which Luke is attempting to describe in Acts 15. The basic issue is the same. The principal participants are the same. But the details of the discussion are quite different. And the decision is stated differently. According to Galatians, James and Peter and John, recognizing that Paul had a divine commission to preach to the Gentiles, agreed that he and Barnabas would be free to work in that field, while they would work with the circumcised Christians. The only stipulation was that the Gentile churches should "remember the poor" (Gal. 2:10).

The whole chronology of Paul's life is involved in this problem. It is sometimes suggested that Galatians 2 reflects an earlier visit to Jerusalem, such as the one recorded in Acts 11:29-30; or that Luke may have recorded one visit as two separate visits. Or it is said that Galatians 2 records a private conference that preceded the public meeting in Acts 15. The text of the Jerusalem decree is studied minutely to see if it cannot be made a statement of moral law rather than ceremonial law. It would take volumes even to summarize the discussion that has turned about this problem.

Essentially, three solutions are possible. (1) We can take Acts as the authority, and force Galatians to conform with Acts. (2) We can take Galatians as the authority and either abandon the account in Acts as totally inaccurate or force Acts to conform with Galatians. This is better than the first solution, since Galatians is, after all, written by an actual participant in the debate. (3) We can simply admit that we have two ancient and authoritative accounts which disagree. If we had more information, undoubtedly many of the disagreements would disappear; perhaps all of them could be reconciled. But we do not have more information. The other pieces of the puzzle are lost. To manufacture the missing pieces out of wishes and guesses is a fascinating pastime, but it hardly leads to truth.

The differences between Acts and Galatians are considerable, but it is a distortion to concentrate on them. The agreements are more important than the differences. Both accounts agree on these essential points: (1) The conversion of the Gentiles posed basic theological problems for the Church, including the relation of the Mosaic Law to salvation and the question of table fellowship between Jewish and Gentile Christians. (2) A circumcision party arose in the church at Jerusalem, insisting that circumcision was essential, both for salvation and for table fellowship. (3) Paul and Barnabas conferred with leaders of the Jerusalem church about this problem. (4) Paul and Barnabas were upheld by the Apostles in their main contention: circumcision is not essential for salvation or for table fellowship. (5) In spite of the decision of the conference at Jerusalem, the circumcision issue continued to agitate the Church for a long time.

The Mission to Macedonia and Greece (15:36—18:17)

The Break with Barnabas (15:36-41)

Paul could not remain indefinitely at Antioch. In his mind's eye he kept seeing the new churches of Galatia, facing persecution and perhaps at this time unsettled by the circumcision controversy. So he proposed to Barnabas that they return to their mission field to see how things were going. Barnabas willingly consented, but asked that they take John Mark. Paul refused to take the one who before had "withdrawn from them" and had not "gone with them to the work." Barnabas insisted. Paul became stubborn on his side. The two missionaries broke up completely. The Greek word for their separation is very strong and does not mean a friendly parting. Barnabas took Mark and returned to his native Cyprus. Paul chose Silas, possibly sending to Jerusalem for him (see 15:33). After a farewell ceremony in the church, he took the overland route for Galatia, pausing on the way to visit churches in Syria and Cilicia.

The breakup with Barnabas was truly a distressing incident. Barnabas had secured Paul's reception into the Jerusalem church (see 9:27), had brought him to Antioch (see 11:25), had been with him in the perils of the missionary journey and the pressures of the Jerusalem Council. It is not to Paul's credit that he could become bitter against such a friend. Luke gives an honest picture of Paul's faults as well as his virtues. Moreover, we are grateful to learn that Paul continued to respect Barnabas (see I Cor. 9:6), and that finally he set a new value on Mark (see II Tim. 4:11).

Timothy Joins the Expedition (16:1-5)

By the overland route, Paul reached the Galatian churches in reverse order. First he came to Derbe, then to Lystra. At Lystra, a new member was added to the expedition, a young Christian named Timothy. Timothy presented a peculiar problem. His mother was a Christian Jewess; his father was a Greek, a nonbeliever. Because of his mixed parentage, Timothy had never been circumcised. According to strict Jewish law, the child of a mixed union inherited his mother's nationality. Therefore Timothy was technically a Jew. Paul foresaw endless disputes over this, particularly in the Galatian churches, where the whole situation was well known. So he circumcised Timothy.

Here is a puzzle. Paul had just fought a great battle to establish the principle that circumcision was not necessary, either for salvation or for table fellowship in the Church. Why would he compromise here? One answer is that neither salvation nor table fellowship was at stake here; it was more a matter of erasing the stigma of illegitimacy from Timothy's birth. Paul was ever ready to compromise when no vital principle was at stake (see I Cor. 9:19-23). Even so, this remains one of the more difficult problems in Acts.

As Paul visited his churches, he delivered copies of the Jerusalem decree. Had the circumcision party already been there with their unsettling doctrine? We cannot be sure. But for the present the churches were growing, both in faith and in numbers. Verse 5 is a typical Lukan summary, but it does not seem here to mark a major division in the book.

The Journey Through Asia Minor (16:6-8)

From Lystra, where Timothy joined the expedition, the main highway led to Iconium and Pisidian Antioch, and then straight west to the great city of Ephesus. Ephesus was the capital of the Roman province of Asia. This is not to be confused with the vast continent of Asia, or even with the area known as Asia Minor today. It was simply the westernmost province in Asia Minor. But it was the oldest, richest, and most populous Roman province in the eastern part of the Empire. Now Paul was preparing to claim Asia for Christ. However, in some way, the Holy Spirit made it clear to him that he was not at this time to preach in Asia. So he took another route and reached the Mediterranean Sea at Troas, far to the north of Ephesus.

This detour is described in verses 6-8. There has been almost endless debate about what these verses mean. The root of the difficulty is the double meaning of place names in Asia Minor during the first century. In previous centuries, many rival kingdoms, with constantly shifting borders, had occupied Asia Minor. Such kingdoms were Phrygia, Pisidia, Lycaonia, Galatia, Bithynia, Mysia, and so on. The Romans had combined the former kingdoms into provinces. Thus the province of Galatia included not only the ancient kingdom of Galatia, to the north, but Lycaonia, Pisidia, and part of Phrygia, to the south. And the province of Asia included Mysia, and part of Phrygia, as well as the territory near Ephesus, which had been called Asia for centuries. But the old place names survived, alongside the official Roman names.

The question is whether Luke uses place names in their ancient meaning or with the more modern, Roman meaning. He does not seem to be entirely consistent one way or the other, so each case must be decided by itself. In the case of Paul's detour, the question becomes really important. If Luke is using the old names, then he must mean that Paul journeyed northeast through ancient Phrygia to ancient Galatia. There he may have preached and founded churches in important cities like Ancyra and Tavium, though no details are given here. But if Luke is using the names as the Romans did, he simply means that Paul went through the part of the province of Galatia which had formerly been the kingdom of Phrygia—in other words, the territory around Iconium and Pisidian Antioch. In this case Paul would have revisited these churches and then gone straight north to the border of Bithynia. Being blocked by the Spirit again, he would have turned west and so would have come to Troas. This would be a much shorter and simpler route and would mean that Paul never visited the ancient kingdom of Galatia at all.

If we could definitely decide Paul's route here, it would settle the much debated question: to whom was the Letter to the Galatians addressed? If Luke and Paul used the ancient place names, then the letter must have gone to churches in Ancyra and Tavium, churches about which we know almost nothing. But if Luke and Paul used the Roman place names, then the letter went to the churches of the first missionary journey: Pisidian Antioch, Iconium, Lystra, and Derbe. The majority of authorities today favor the latter view.

The Call to Macedonia (16:9-10)

At Troas Paul had a vision. A man was pleading with him to cross the Aegean Sea to Macedonia. In ancient times, Macedonia had been the home of Alexander the Great. Now it was a Roman province of major importance, straddling the main highway from the east to Rome. The period of indecision was now ended. The missionaries accepted Paul's vision as the call of God.

It is easy to put too much emphasis on the fact that Macedonia was in Europe. The line between Europe and Asia was not an important one in the first century. The Aegean Sea was "a Greek lake," and the culture on its eastern shores, in Asia Minor, was every bit as "European" as the culture on its western shores, in Macedonia and Greece. It is significant, however, that the gospel was definitely moving west. If Paul had been permitted to go into Bithynia and onward to the east, Europeans and Americans might be hearing the gospel today from the lips of Japanese and Indian missionaries, rather than the other way around.

It is notable that the first "we" appears in verse 10 (see the Introduction). Does this mean that Luke joined the expedition at Troas? That is the most natural interpretation, though he may have been with them all along. It has been suggested that Luke was a Macedonian physician who was temporarily at Troas. Being summoned to treat Paul's recurring ailment, he had been converted. Long into the night he pleaded with Paul to take the gospel to Macedonia. After he left, Paul went to sleep and had the vision of the man from Macedonia. That is an intriguing suggestion, but it cannot be proved.

The Beginning of the Mission to Philippi (16:11-15)

The winds were very favorable, and the voyage to Macedonia was completed in two days, with a stop at the island of Samothrace. The missionaries went directly from Neapolis, the seaport, to Philippi, a major city and a Roman colony. Paul's strategy called for establishing the Church first in important centers, from which the gospel could be spread into surrounding territory.

His strategy also called for an appeal to the Jews first. But in Philippi there were not enough Jews to form a synagogue. Accordingly, on the Sabbath the missionaries went outside the gates to the riverside, hoping to find a small Jewish gathering there. They were not disappointed. A group of women were gathered for prayer. Among them was Lydia, a Gentile from Thyatira, apparently a widow who made her living by selling the purple goods for which Thyatira was famous. Attracted by the Jewish Scriptures, she was already a God-fearer. She became the first convert in Macedonia. When she was baptized, her whole household was baptized with her, including, presumably, her children and her servants. In ancient Israel, family solidarity had been strong. God's Covenant had always involved the whole family, children and servants included (see Gen. 17). In the New Israel this same feeling prevailed, and baptism was often by households (see Acts 16:33; I Cor. 1:16). Lydia's house became headquarters for the missionaries as long as they were in Philippi.

The Healing of the Slave Girl (16:16-18)

One day, on the way to the place of prayer, the missionaries were met by a slave girl who was possessed by an unclean spirit. Demon possession was a common phenomenon in the ancient world, as any reader of the Gospels knows. A modern reporter might describe the slave girl as mentally ill; but to her contemporaries it seemed that another personality—a clever, evil spirit —had invaded her body and controlled her. She was enabled by her condition to go into a trance and to mumble apparent predictions of the future. The men who owned her were quick to turn this to gain.

It was typical of those possessed by unclean spirits that contact with persons possessed by the Holy Spirit threw them into a frenzy, so that they cried out, acknowledging the superior Power (see Mark 1:24; 3:11; 5:7; 9:20). When this had happened repeatedly, Paul turned and, in the name of Jesus Christ, commanded the spirit to leave her. The cure was immediate.

Paul and Silas Jailed (16:19-24)

Instead of rejoicing at the healing of a human being, the girl's owners mourned the loss of their profits. They seized Paul and Silas and dragged them before the local officials. Luke first calls them "rulers"—a general term. Then he more precisely identifies them as "magistrates." The Latin equivalent is "praetors." We know from inscriptions that the magistrates of Roman colonies were often called "praetors," as a courtesy title. Charges could be made to these officials by any citizen. The charges made by the owners had nothing to do with the curing of the girl; they were exceedingly vague—that Paul and Silas disturbed the city and advocated unlawful customs. But the charges were worded so as to appeal to the powerful motives of race prejudice ("These men are Jews") and civic pride ("us Romans"). A mob soon formed. Without further trial, the magistrates stripped Paul and Silas and ordered them beaten with rods. After the beating, they were taken to the local jail and placed in the innermost prison, with their feet in the stocks.

The Conversion of the Jailer (16:25-34)

Here is the third miraculous escape from prison in Acts (see 5:19-21 and 12:6-11). Is the escape more miraculous than the

courage and supernatural joy which enabled men who had been
punished for doing good, men whose backs were still a bloody
pulp, men who had few friends and many enemies, to sing hymns
at midnight amid the nauseous odors and damp darkness of a
common prison? An earthquake came, shaking all doors open
and all fetters loose. The jailer thought all his prisoners had escaped, and determined to commit suicide since he would surely
be executed for his negligence (see 12:19). A timely reassurance
from Paul prevented him. He called for lights, rushed in, brought
Paul and Silas out, and asked: "Men, what must I do to be
saved?"

It is difficult to know what the jailer meant by his question. He
had confronted death and the loss of honor, and he was still ter-
ribly upset. This could be seen in the way he rushed about, the
way he trembled with fear, the way he fell down before Paul and
Silas. Perhaps he was still wondering if he could really escape
execution and dishonor when morning came.

But a man who faces death always faces in some sense the
judgment of God. The jailer was a pagan and his fears of final
judgment may have been unformed and unspoken. But it was to
those ultimate fears that Paul and Silas spoke: "Believe in the
Lord Jesus, and you will be saved, you and your household."
This has been called the shortest statement of the way of salvation. Paul and Silas had to amplify it (vs. 32), but the nub is
there. The whole setting makes it plain that the belief which saves
is not mere intellectual acceptance of facts—the jailer was not
interested in that when his life was at stake; it is trembling trust
in One who can deliver because he is Lord.

The jailer gave evidence of his surrender to a new Lord when
he tenderly washed his prisoners' wounds (he had not bothered
about them before); when he took them into his own house; and
when he fed them. Again there was a household baptism. It was
performed at night, either in the jail or in the jailer's house. This
makes it questionable whether there was any one set mode of baptism in New Testament times. The marvelous joy of the Spirit
(vs. 34; compare 8:8, 39; 13:52) confirmed the water-baptism.

The Magistrates Apologize (16:35-40)

Early the next morning the magistrates (praetors) sent the
police (lictors) with orders to release Paul and Silas. Apparently
the magistrates realized the flimsy nature of the charges against

them; possibly they had jailed them mainly for protection against the mob. At this point, we discover a fact Luke has not mentioned before: both Paul and Silas were Roman citizens! When the city of Rome was conquering all the lands about the Mediterranean, there was a great distinction between the citizens of Rome and the citizens of the conquered lands. Under the Empire, this distinction continued. A citizen of Rome had rights and privileges that the mass of citizens of the Empire did not possess. Since Philippi was a Roman colony, the Philippians possessed the privileges of Roman citizens (see 16:21). How Paul had obtained Roman citizenship appears later (see 22:22-29).

On this occasion he used his citizenship to teach the Philippian magistrates a lesson. He demanded that they come personally and release him and Silas. This they did with great apologies. We may wonder why Paul had not used his citizenship to prevent the beating in the first place, or to avoid the stoning he had suffered at Lystra (see 14:19). In the face of furious mob action there may have been no opportunity to establish the facts.

After a visit to Lydia and a final exhortation to the church, the missionaries left Philippi, to the great relief of the magistrates. Apparently Luke stayed on, for the "we" does not appear again until Paul returns to Philippi (see 20:5-6).

The Mission to Thessalonica (17:1-9)

Leaving Philippi, Paul and his companions traveled along the Via Egnatia, a famous Roman road. Amphipolis and Apollonia were well-known Macedonian cities, but Paul pressed on to Thessalonica, the capital of Macedonia. In this large city there were enough Jews to form a synagogue, so Paul followed his usual strategy and began his preaching there, speaking on three successive Sabbaths. Luke gives a compact summary of what Paul preached: (1) The Scriptures prove that the Messiah was to suffer and to rise from the dead; (2) Jesus suffered and was raised; (3) therefore Jesus is the Messiah. This is a sharpened and developed form of the argument Paul had used in the synagogue at Pisidian Antioch (see 13:16-41). This was his typical approach to the Jews.

The results were also typical: a few Jewish converts, and a larger number from among the God-fearing Gentiles. The Jews grew jealous, stirred up a mob, and attacked the house of Jason, where the missionaries were staying. When they could not find the missionaries, they dragged Jason and some of the new Christians before the city authorities. We know from inscriptions that in Thessalonica the local magistrates were called "politarchs," and that is the word Luke uses. The charge against Jason was that he had received into his house dangerous revolutionaries—"men who have turned the world upside down." It was further charged that all the Christians were disobeying the decrees of Caesar by setting up Jesus as another king or emperor (see the comment on 2:33-36).

These charges raise some serious questions. Christianity began as a revolutionary movement. Its enemies could say with considerable justice that Christians were out to turn the world upside down. We do not hear such charges today. The world is in fact being turned upside down in one of the greatest revolutions of all time. But the Church, instead of leading the revolution into constructive, Christian channels, is all too often on the side of conservative and even reactionary forces. Are we being true to our heritage? Again, is our loyalty to Christ as Lord and King so great that the forces in our society that demand ultimate loyalty—state, party, race, social set, or whatever—are disturbed about it? Or is it evident to all that our loyalty to Christ comes second to many other things?

The politarchs were disturbed. But since the principal revolutionaries could not be found, they did not immediately prosecute Jason and the rest. They released them on bond. Whether they were subsequently tried and punished, Luke does not tell us. From I Thessalonians 2:14-16, we would judge that in one way or another they suffered for their faith.

The Mission to Beroea (17:10-15)

For the protection of their converts, Paul and Silas had to be sent out of town at once. So they left by night and went on to Beroea. Here the success of the gospel among the Jews was so great that Luke makes special note of it. But when opposition failed to arise locally, it soon arrived from Thessalonica. Paul was the main target, so he was sent on to Athens, which was out of Macedonia altogether. Silas and Timothy managed to stay on to strengthen the Macedonian work, but not for long, for Paul sent back orders that they must join him as soon as possible.

Paul at Athens (17:16-21)

Paul found himself, contrary to his previous plans, in the province of Achaia, or Greece, and in the city of Athens. Even then, the glories of Athens lay in the past, a past as remote to Paul as the days of the Renaissance and the Reformation are to us. Corinth had outstripped Athens as the political and commercial center of Greece. But Athens was still the center of Greek culture, crowded with temples and statues and other relics of its great past, and was the scene of daily debates among the philosophers.

Paul may not have intended to preach there at all, but the rampant idolatry of the place aroused his fighting spirit. He began a double ministry: each Sabbath he argued in the synagogue with the Jews and their Gentile adherents; each weekday he spoke to all comers in the market place—a custom which had been traditional in Athens from the days of Socrates. Here the Epicurean and Stoic philosophers also debated. Paul's encounter with them drew a crowd.

The crowd could not understand Paul very well, but they caught the words "Iesous" (Jesus) and "Anastasis" (resurrection). Some mocked him as a babbler or worthless fellow. Some supposed that he was preaching a new mystery religion from the East, perhaps one with a male and a female deity. The confusion grew so great that he was carried before the Areopagus for an investigation of his teaching. Originally, "the Areopagus" was a place name for Mars' Hill, a prominent hill in Athens. There, in the days of Athens' glory, all murder trials were held. Later, however, "the Areopagus" came to mean not the place but the court which met there. In Paul's day, this court was the chief local authority in Athens. It was particularly charged with maintaining order in the market place. It met no longer on the hill, but in a "Stoa" or columned porch, just off the market place. Before this court Paul was brought, not so much on a specific charge as out of curiosity. Luke cannot refrain from poking fun at this well-known characteristic of the Athenians (see vs. 21).

Paul's Speech Before the Areopagus (17:22-34)

Paul addressed one of his most interesting sermons to the Athenian court. His point of departure was an inscription on an Athenian altar, "To an unknown god." It seems well established that there were such altars at Athens, though they probably read:

"To unknown gods," that is, to any other gods who might exist and whom men ought to avoid offending. Paul's point is that, for all their gods, the Athenians have not known the one true God. In verses 24-27, he makes the following points about the true God: (1) He created all things; (2) he does not live in temples made by men; (3) men do not provide for his wants, but he for theirs; (4) he is not the property of one nation, but has created all nations from a single stock, that all may seek him. Thus far, the sermon is thoroughly Jewish. Although the Old Testament is not quoted, echoes of its language are everywhere. The theology is straight from its pages: God's unity, his creation and maintenance of all things, his control of all history.

Paul next makes the point that the Athenians should have known the Unknown God after all. He is not far from any man. Even their own poets have spoken of a great God in whom "we live and move and have our being," and have said that "we are indeed his offspring." The first quotation seems to be from a lost poem of Epimenides, a legendary wise man of Crete. The second comes rather surely from Aratus, who was from Paul's home province of Cilicia, and who wrote a long poem about astronomy. The use of these quotations does not necessarily prove that Paul was specially versed in Greek literature. Many quotations pass into popular speech, much as men today quote Shakespeare without being aware of the source of their quotation. It is significant, however, that Paul does use pagan material, with which his hearers were familiar, rather than the Old Testament, which they did not know. He gathers his quotations into an attack on their idolatry. Men who are the offspring of God, he says, ought to have better sense than to worship images (vs. 29).

In verses 30-31, we reach the distinctively Christian part of Paul's message. A new moment in time has arrived, he declares. The true God will no longer overlook the ignorance of the Gentiles. All men everywhere must repent, because the Day of Judgment has now been fixed and a man has been appointed as judge. This is no finespun theory, but a fact which God has made known to all men by raising from the dead that very man who is to be judge. Paul uses "man" here as more understandable to a Gentile audience than the Jewish expression "Son of man" which Jesus so often used in predicting the Judgment and also the Resurrection (see Luke 9:22, 26; 17:22-37; 18:31-33; 21:27, 36; 22:69).

At this point Paul was interrupted by raucous laughter. He

probably could have stood a shower of stones better. The idea of
resurrection was ludicrous to the sophisticated Athenians, but to
Paul it was the great essential of the good news he had to tell. It
should be noted that the doctrine of the immortality of the soul
was well known at Athens and would have occasioned no jeers.
But resurrection of the body was an offense. How has it come
about that modern Christians hardly know there is a distinction
between the two and tend to stand with the Athenians rather than
with Paul?

There were some there who wanted to hear Paul again. A small
group joined themselves to Paul and after further instruction became believers. One of them, named Dionysius, was a member of
the Areopagus itself, and another was a woman named Damaris.
It is uncertain whether there were enough converts to form a
church at that time.

Of all the speeches in Acts, this one has been most widely discussed. Some interpreters have maintained that Paul could not
have possibly made such a speech, so different is it from the
thought of his letters and from the tenor of his preaching as recorded elsewhere in Acts. Yet when we remember that this is the
only full account we have of a speech by Paul to a totally pagan
audience, and when we compare it with the beginning of another
such speech (see 14:15-17), these objections are greatly reduced.
There is really nothing here that Paul could not have said, and
much that he surely would have said to such an audience.

Others have granted that Paul preached in this way at Athens.
But, they say, it was a mistake which he greatly regretted. In this
view, Paul was a failure in Athens because he tried to accommo-
date the gospel to Greek philosophy; as a result, when he went to
Corinth, he decided to preach nothing "except Jesus Christ and
him crucified" (I Cor. 2:2). This is reading too much between
the lines. It is true that Paul found Athens a poor seedbed for the
gospel. But there is no real evidence that he regretted the line of
preaching he had taken. Some were converted by it, which is an
indication that he had the Spirit's blessing.

Paul Reaches Corinth (18:1-4)

Paul left Athens—the Greek hints that he may have been ordered to leave—and went to Corinth. The ancient Greek city had
been destroyed almost two centuries before this, and in its place
a Roman colony had been built by Julius Caesar. It was made the

capital of Achaia. Cargoes were often unloaded on one side of
the narrow isthmus on which Corinth stood, transported by land,
and reloaded on the other side, to save the difficult and dangerous
voyage around the lower end of Greece. This made Corinth a
commercial center, and it rapidly grew into the largest city of the
province. It had the dubious fame of being the most wicked city
in the Roman Empire.

Here Paul met a Jewish couple who were destined to be among
his closest friends for the rest of his life: Aquila and Priscilla.
Formerly they had been residents of Rome, where there was a
large and influential Jewish colony. Recently they had been expelled from Rome by the Emperor Claudius. Suetonius, a Roman
historian, refers to the fact that Claudius expelled the Jews from
Rome because they were creating a great tumult about one
"Chrestus." Very probably this means that the first Christians had
reached Rome and that, as usual, conflict arose between them and
the Jews. Claudius, unable to distinguish between Jewish Christians and the regular Jews of the synagogue, simply banished all
Jews from Rome. The banishment was only temporary, and probably many of the Jews never left at all. This incident can be dated
around A.D. 49.

Paul made his home with Aquila and Priscilla, and the three
of them worked together at the tentmakers' trade, which included
leatherwork as well. Luke has not told us before how Paul supported himself. Every Jewish boy learned a trade, and Paul had
evidently learned his in Tarsus, which was famous for its cloth
of goats' hair. Paul had supported himself thus at Thessalonica
(see I Thess. 2:9), and probably elsewhere on his travels. No record is given of the conversion of Aquila and Priscilla, yet they
appear later as Christians (see 18:26; Rom. 16:3-5). The best
explanation is that they had been converted already in Rome. We
can imagine that as they worked they talked about the church in
Rome, and that Paul's intense longing to visit Rome dates from
this point. In the meantime, he began to witness, as usual, in the
synagogue every Sabbath.

Paul Leaves the Synagogue (18:5-11)

Silas and Timothy arrived from Macedonia, possibly bringing
some aid which gave Paul more time for preaching (see Phil.
4:15). From I Thessalonians 3:1-2, we learn that Timothy had
been sent back to Thessalonica from Athens, a fact which Luke

does not mention. The probable course of events was this: (1) Paul went to Athens alone; (2) Timothy and Silas met him there; (3) their report of the persecutions in Macedonia led Paul to send them back; (4) Paul moved on to Corinth; (5) they rejoined him there. Paul continued to keep in touch with the Macedonian churches from Corinth. First and Second Thessalonians were written there.

As Paul kept insisting that the Messiah was Jesus, the Jews in the synagogue opposed and reviled him. Once again, as in Pisidian Antioch, Paul formally and ceremoniously turned to the Gentiles. He moved out of the synagogue and into the home of a Roman named Titius Justus, who lived next door. This must have been exceedingly irritating to the Jews, since Titius Justus was originally their convert, a God-fearer. To make matters worse, Crispus, the ruler of the synagogue, was converted and took his whole family next door, to the Christian church. For eighteen months Paul, encouraged by a vision, made convert after convert among the Corinthians.

Paul Before Gallio (18:12-17)

Finally the Jews could stand it no longer and brought Paul before Gallio, the proconsul of Achaia. From secular records we know that Gallio, brother of the famous writer Seneca, was proconsul of Achaia from A.D. 51 to 52, and was possibly in office one year before or after that. The charge brought by the Jews was strictly religious, without the usual political overtones. Before Paul could speak in his defense, Gallio dismissed the case, refusing to judge a matter of the Jewish religion. With typical Roman arrogance, he had the protesting Jews driven from the tribunal.

This was followed by the beating of Sosthenes. Several interpretations of this are possible. (1) Sosthenes was a Jew, appointed to take Crispus' place as ruler of the synagogue. His fellow Jews, frustrated at the poor success of their case, vented their anger on him. Or, as some manuscripts have it, the Greeks, disgusted with all Jews, beat him. (2) Sosthenes was a Christian. Either Crispus had Sosthenes as another name, or a second ruler of the synagogue had been converted. The Jews, unable to punish Paul, beat up one of his converts. First Corinthians 1:1 lends support to this. In either case, Gallio paid no attention to the beating.

The Mission to Ephesus (18:18—19:20)

Paul's Preliminary Visit (18:18-23)

Following the trial before Gallio, Paul stayed on at Corinth for an indefinite period; but already his eyes were turned toward another great center. Just across the Aegean Sea, in frequent communication with Corinth, lay Ephesus, the capital of the rich province of Asia. Ephesus had been his goal when he left Antioch years before (see the comment on 16:6-8), and now he felt that the Spirit no longer barred him from working there.

Taking Priscilla and Aquila with him, he bade farewell to the church at Corinth and took ship at the port of Cenchreae. There he cut his hair in connection with a vow. From early times there had been among the Jews an order of Nazirites, holy men who drank no wine and never cut their hair (see Judges 13:4-5; Amos 2:11-12; Luke 1:15). There was also the provision for a man or a woman to be a temporary Nazirite, for a limited period of time (see Num. 6:1-21). Paul had apparently taken a vow to be a Nazirite as long as he was in Corinth.

From Cenchreae, they sailed straight to Ephesus. Paul left Priscilla and Aquila there, apparently to lay the foundations of Christian work. He himself made an opening address in the synagogue. But he could not stay at that time. Instead, he sailed away to Caesarea, went from there to Antioch, revisited the churches in Galatia and Phrygia, and finally reached Ephesus again by the overland route which he had found blocked on his previous journey (see 19:1; compare 16:6).

Luke gives few details of this long trip, and no explanation of why it was taken. In some manuscripts Paul explains in the words, "I must by all means keep this feast that cometh in Jerusalem." The expression in verse 22, "he went up and greeted the church," would then be understood as a visit to Jerusalem. Another possibility is that Paul could not feel himself completely absolved from his vow until he made certain sacrifices at Jerusalem (compare 21:26). Still another possibility is that word reached Paul at Ephesus that the circumcision party was causing trouble in Galatia (see Gal. 1:6), and he felt obliged to visit that field again before settling in Ephesus. But his route was certainly the long way around. This journey remains a mystery.

Apollos at Ephesus (18:24-28)

While Paul was making the circuit to Caesarea and back, Apollos visited Ephesus. He was a Jew from Alexandria, a great center of Jewish culture and literature. His language had the polished eloquence of the schools, and he was an authority on the Old Testament. Was he a Christian when he arrived? The weight of the evidence shows that he was. (1) There is no indication that Aquila and Priscilla baptized him, though Luke could have omitted this. (2) He had been instructed in the Way, which surely means Christian instruction. (3) His teaching about Jesus is described as accurate. (4) He had the gift of the Holy Spirit, for the words "being fervent in spirit" do not describe a natural temperament, but rather a "boiling-over" with the Holy Spirit (compare the same expression in Rom. 12:11). He had also the ability to "speak boldly," which is one of the notable gifts of the Spirit (see 4:13, 29, 31; 9:27; 13:46; 14:3; 19:8).

Nevertheless, Apollos' Christianity was imperfect. Priscilla and Aquila, after hearing him, felt he needed further instruction, which they gave him. The only clue to what was lacking is in the words: "he knew only the baptism of John." How difficult it is to understand what that means will appear better after studying the next section (see the comment on 19:1-7). After being instructed, Apollos was sent by the brethren across the Aegean to Achaia. This indicates that Aquila and Priscilla had already gathered a small group of converts ("brethren") at Ephesus. In Achaia, Apollos had a fruitful ministry, proclaiming, as Paul had done before him, that "the Christ was Jesus" (compare vs. 28 with 18:5). He was especially popular at Corinth, where his intense admirers almost divided the church (see I Cor. 1:12; 3:4-6). It has been suggested that Apollos was the author of the Letter to the Hebrews, but that cannot be proved.

The Twelve Ephesian Disciples (19:1-7)

After Apollos had left, Paul arrived and surveyed the situation at Ephesus. He found disciples there. His first question was most significant: "Did you receive the Holy Spirit when you believed?" In Acts the presence and power of the Holy Spirit are the distinctive marks of the Church. Where these are found, the Church exists. Peter had pointed to the Spirit to prove that the church at Caesarea must be recognized (see 11:15-18). Paul and Barnabas used the same argument to prove that there were churches among the Gentiles (see 15:12). What is the mark of the Church? This question has become acute in our own day, as the ecumenical movement strives to express more clearly our unity in Christ. We look for bishops in the proper succession, or for a proper view of Scripture, before we will acknowledge other bodies as the Church. Ought we not first of all to be looking for signs of the Spirit's working?

The answer of the Ephesian disciples was: "We have never even heard that there is a Holy Spirit." How many modern churches does that describe! The real measure of the difference between the Early Church and the Church today is this: they were acutely conscious of the Spirit as the secret of their inner life and the power for their witnessing; we frequently act as though we have not heard that there is a Holy Spirit.

Paul then asked about their baptism. The clear implication is that if they had been properly baptized, they would have received the Spirit. They replied that they had been baptized into John's baptism. This may mean that they had actually been baptized, years before, by John the Baptist himself. It is more likely, however, that there existed, alongside Christianity in its early years, a movement of John's followers. These men did not know about Jesus, or did not recognize him as the Messiah whom John had promised. So they were still calling men to repentance, still promising them that the Messiah would come, still baptizing them into the community of those who awaited the Coming One (see the comment on 2:37-40, 41-42).

When Paul explained to them that the Messiah whom they awaited had already come, they were baptized again, this time in the name of the Lord Jesus. Paul laid his hands on them (see 8:17) and the Holy Spirit came, evidencing his presence by the gifts of tongues (see the comment on 2:5-13) and prophecy (see the comment on 11:27-30).

There must be some connection between these disciples and Apollos. He, like them, "knew only the baptism of John" (see 18:25). And the emphasis of Apollos' preaching, after he had been further instructed, was that the Messiah is Jesus (see 18:28), which is exactly the instruction Paul gave to the twelve men. Yet Apollos appears as a Christian, possessing the Spirit, needing no further baptism. Apparently the instruction he received before reaching Ephesus made that difference (see 18:25). How much mystery still surrounds Acts, and, in particular, the relation between Spirit-baptism and water-baptism! Yet in spite of the mystery, this story, more clearly than any other, seems to teach that, normally, the two baptisms belong together. They are two sides of one great action of God, whereby men are brought into the Church, the Body of Christ (see the comment on 8:14-25).

Paul Leaves the Synagogue (19:8-10)

The pattern set in Pisidian Antioch (see 13:13-52) and Corinth (see 18:1-17) was now followed at Ephesus. Paul began with bold preaching in the synagogue about the Kingdom of God (see the comment on 1:3-5). Some of the Jews opposed him, so he took his disciples with him and moved to the hall of Tyrannus. This was probably a hall regularly used by philosophers and other lecturers. We do not know whether Tyrannus was the owner of the hall or was the lecturer who regularly spoke there. A curious reading in some of the manuscripts indicates that Paul used the hall "from the fifth hour to the tenth." This would be from 11:00 A.M. to 4:00 P.M., the hours when most of the population took a long midday siesta. During regular working hours in the early morning and late afternoon, Paul probably worked at his trade.

For two years, Paul continued his daily preaching in Ephesus. They were extremely eventful years. He carried on an extensive correspondence with the church at Corinth, and paid them one hurried visit. He also suffered considerable persecution (see I Cor. 15:32; II Cor. 1:8). Some scholars believe that Paul was imprisoned at Ephesus, and that Philippians, Colossians, and Philemon were written during that imprisonment. The evidence for this is too slender to win general agreement.

Luke is content to summarize the general results of Paul's ministry at Ephesus: "all the residents of Asia heard the word of the Lord, both Jews and Greeks." Paul, with masterful strategy, had chosen Ephesus as his preaching center because it was the key to the whole province of Asia (see the comment on 16:6-8). All Asia came to Ephesus to trade and to worship in the temple of Artemis. Paul did not have to take long, hard journeys from city to city throughout Asia. The daily lectures in the hall of Tyrannus were a center of Christian infection. From Smyrna, and Pergamum, and Thyatira, and Sardis, and Philadelphia, and Laodicea, and Colossae, and Hierapolis men came to Ephesus, heard Paul, and went back to found the churches of Asia.

The Gospel Triumphs (19:11-20)

Luke seems to have had a special interest in the conflict between the Christian gospel and the superstition and magic that infested the ancient world. He tells of Peter and Simon (8:9-24), Paul and Bar-Jesus (13:4-12), and now of Paul and Asian magic. Paul's power to heal and cast out demons must have seemed magical to the Asians (compare the "magic" of Peter in 5:15-16). Exorcism—casting out unclean spirits—was attempted widely by magicians of that day, who used incantations or "spells" to drive the demons out. Ephesus was a center for this, and books of Ephesian "spells" were sold all over the world. Renegade Jews traveled about as professional exorcists. Such a group came to Ephesus, claiming to be sons of the high priest. Actually, "Sceva" was never a high priest. These fakers heard Paul exorcise an evil spirit in the name of Jesus. Understanding this as a "spell," they repeated the name. The results were tragic and also ridiculous: the demon-possessed man beat up the exorcists. As word of this spread, many of the believers who had been deeply infected by magic and superstition, and were secretly holding on to their charms and books, now made a clean break and burned the relics of their superstition. This same struggle and victory can be witnessed on the mission fields even today.

Verse 20 is another of Luke's summaries. It almost surely marks the real end of Paul's ministry in Ephesus.

The Journey to Jerusalem (19:21—21:14)

Preparations for the Journey (19:21-22)

Led by the Spirit, Paul planned to leave Ephesus, revisit his churches in Macedonia and Achaia, go to Jerusalem, and then journey to Rome. A glance at the map will show what a roundabout journey Paul was proposing for himself. The route by which Paul left Ephesus seems as much a mystery as the route by which he came there (see 18:18-23). But this time his letters provide the key.

The growing rift between the Jewish and Gentile wings of the Church was a matter of deep concern to Paul. It became his dream to heal that rift in a very practical way. He would collect from his Gentile churches a gift of money for the church at Jerusalem, which was in continuous financial trouble. This gift would be tangible testimony that, all disputing about circumcision aside, Jews and Gentiles are one body in Christ. It would renew the close sharing in the Spirit that had marked the early days of the Church (see 4:32-35). It would follow the pattern laid down by the church at Antioch (see 11:27-30). It would carry out Paul's agreement with the leaders at Jerusalem (see Gal. 2:10). From Ephesus he had already sent out letters about the gift (see I Cor. 16:1-4). Now he sent agents to help the local churches collect the money. He planned to follow close behind them for the final gathering of the funds. Then, with delegates from the churches, he would deliver the gift to Jerusalem. Only when that responsibility was discharged would he feel free to go to that city which for some time had been drawing him like a magnet—Rome itself!

The Riot at Ephesus (19:23-41)

As Paul prepares to leave Ephesus, Luke finally mentions the most outstanding feature of the religious life of that great city— the worship of Artemis. Artemis of the Ephesians was an ancient oriental goddess of fertility. The Greeks who settled Asia gave her the name Artemis, or Diana, identifying her with their chaste goddess of the hunt; but her ancient oriental nature remained unchanged. She is usually pictured in oriental garb and covered with many breasts, the symbol of her fertility.

The great temple at Ephesus, built in her honor, was about four times the size of the Parthenon at Athens. It was a masterpiece of Greek architecture, adorned with masterpieces of Greek sculpture. It was considered one of the seven wonders of the ancient world. It was a major tourist attraction, an asylum for escaped criminals and slaves, and the bank for all of Asia. Ephesus had outstripped many rival cities to become the capital of Asia.

The silversmiths of Ephesus were one of many groups which profited enormously from the presence of the temple of Artemis. They made little silver souvenirs, for which visitors to the city and worshipers of Artemis paid a handsome price. The preaching of Paul had caused a definite decline in sales. A man named Demetrius gathered his fellow silversmiths together and stirred them up to attack Paul. Demetrius' recipe for stirring up a riot can hardly be improved on: (1) Appeal basically to the love of gain; (2) then hide that appeal behind an appeal to patriotism and religion, so that the rioter no longer sees his real motives, but becomes a hero in his own eyes.

Whipped into a frenzy by Demetrius' shrewd manipulation, the silversmiths started the cry: "Great is Artemis of the Ephesians!" It echoed through all the twisted alleys of the city and brought a huge and confused crowd out to the theater. This theater, which has been excavated, could easily have held 25,000 people. A mob needs victims, and they soon located two of Paul's traveling companions. They did not find Paul, but he would have come voluntarily to face the crowd if his disciples and the Asiarchs had not insisted otherwise. The Asiarchs were the leading men of the whole province of Asia. Some, perhaps all, of them had served as high priests of the Asian *Concilia,* a league of Asian cities organized for the purpose of emperor worship. In an aside, Luke indicates that Paul had close friends in this group. How we would like to hear the story of that friendship and how it started!

Utter confusion reigned in the theater. The Jews became involved. Their spokesman Alexander was unable to make his defense. As in the case of Sosthenes before Gallio (see 18:12-17), it is not clear whether Alexander was seeking to defend Paul or to defend the Jews in general.

Finally, after two hours of pandemonium, the town clerk restored order. Other records of Ephesus mention this official; he kept the records of all assemblies of the citizens, and was the executive who enforced all local ordinances. In a very sensible speech he reminds the Ephesians that their world-wide reputation as the seat of the worship of Artemis has not really been destroyed. He alludes to something that fell from the sky—possibly a meteorite which was considered a relic of Artemis. Then he declares that the Christians have not been blasphemous in attacking the Ephesian worship. He points out that there are such things as courts and proconsuls for the settlement of disputes between individuals. And there are regular assemblies of all free citizens to discuss matters of importance to the whole city. But such an irregular assembly as they had held endangered their right to assemble at all. The crowd was dismissed. Clearly the time had come for Paul to leave Ephesus.

The Visit to Macedonia and Greece (20:1-6)

A tremendous amount of travel is here crowded into a few words. From Paul's letters we can supply some additional details. After the riot, he left Ephesus and revisited his Macedonian churches. There Titus met him with good news from the church at Corinth, which prompted Paul to write Second Corinthians, or at least part of it (see II Cor. 7:5-7). Paul was further encouraged by the marvelous liberality of the Macedonians in contributing to the relief fund (see II Cor. 8:1-5). At length Paul arrived in Greece, where he spent three months at Corinth. It was at this time that he probably wrote the Letter to the Romans (see Rom. 15:23-33).

From Corinth Paul planned to sail straight across to Syria, in order to reach Jerusalem in time for the Feast of the Passover. However, he learned of a Jewish plot—perhaps Jewish pilgrims planned to murder him on the boat. So he retraced his steps into Macedonia. Luke pauses here to list Paul's traveling companions, men appointed by the churches to go with him to deliver the gift. Sopater and Secundus are mentioned only here. Aristarchus had been a victim of the mob at Ephesus (see 19:29); he later accompanied Paul to Rome (see 27:2) and helped him there (see Philemon 24). At some time he was Paul's fellow prisoner (see Col. 4:10). Gaius of Derbe is probably not the same as Gaius the Macedonian who was dragged with Aristarchus before the Ephesian mob (see 19:29); Gaius was a very common name. Timothy had been Paul's constant helper since he joined the missionaries at Lystra (see 16:1-3). Tychicus was later the bearer of the Letters to the Ephesians and the Colossians (see Eph. 6:21 and Col. 4:7). Trophimus was soon to be the occasion of Paul's arrest in Jerusalem (see 21:29). Those who picture Paul as a hard, forbidding character will have difficulty in explaining this devoted circle of friends, most of whom remained loyal to the very end (see II Tim. 4:9, 12, 20).

These companions went on to Troas, but Paul stayed in Philippi to observe the Passover ("the days of Unleavened Bread") there. At this point, the "we" reappears. Probably Luke had remained in Philippi ever since Paul left there at the request of the praetors (see 16:11-40). The winds were unfavorable, and it took five days' sailing to reach Troas (compare the swift voyage in 16:11-12). They stayed there a week.

Paul at Troas (20:7-12)

This little story gives us a number of precious insights into the life of the Early Church. The customary meeting time was the evening of the first day of the week. This was the time when the Risen Lord had met with his disciples to break bread (see Luke

24:13-43; John 20:19-29). Still he met with them as they broke bread together (see the comment on 2:43-47). The Lord's Supper was thus the living center of Christian worship. It was accompanied by the preaching of the Word. The Christians had no church buildings, and worshiped in homes. There seems to have been a preference for upper rooms, perhaps in memory of the first Lord's Supper. Everyone brought a torch, or candle, to make the room bright with light.

On this occasion the sermon was long and the many flickering lights made it hard to keep one's eyes open. A young man named Eutychus dozed off in the window where he was sitting and fell three floors to the street outside. The worshipers dashed down and picked him up. Paul came down, embraced him, and pronounced that his life was still in him. If by "taken up dead" (vs. 9) Luke means he was really dead, then this is to be understood as another miracle, similar to the raising of Dorcas (see 9:36-43). But if these words indicate only the assumption of those who lifted Eutychus, then Luke does not indicate anything more than that the young man was stunned and had his breath knocked out.

The sacrament had not yet been observed, so the church reassembled for that. Then Paul continued to talk until daybreak, while Eutychus was led home to recuperate.

The Voyage to Miletus (20:13-16)

Now begins the detailed record of Paul's travels that lasts, with time out for some speeches, for the rest of Acts. We are told each place he stopped, and the number of days' travel between stops. Almost surely this is based on a log or diary kept by Luke. A glance at a good map will be more helpful here than pages of commentary.

Paul walked overland to Assos, boarded the ship there, and stayed aboard until it reached Miletus. Miletus is a port near Ephesus, and there they were delayed for a while. Paul did not dare go to Ephesus himself. He had missed the opportunity of presenting his gift at the Passover, and he was determined to reach Jerusalem in time to make the presentation at Pentecost. If he should go to Ephesus, he would be tempted to stay there too long.

The Farewell to the Ephesian Elders (20:17-38)

So Paul sent to Ephesus, thirty miles away, and asked the officers of the church to come to him at Miletus. In verse 17 they are called "elders" (or presbyters). In verse 28 they are called "guardians" (or bishops). In the next century, these officers were sharply distinguished, and the presbyters were subjected to the authority of the bishops. But at this point, the terms were synonymous (compare Titus 1:5, 7).

Paul's speech to the elders follows no logical order, save the logic of the heart. There are three main themes to which he comes back again and again. The first is a reminder to the Ephesians of his ministry among them. It was a ministry of humility, tears, and trials (vss. 19 and 31); a ministry in which he pulled no punches (vss. 20, 26-27); a ministry of both public teaching and house-to-house visitation (vss. 20 and 31). Its great themes were repentance, faith, and the Kingdom of God (vss. 21 and 25). It had been carried out, not for profit, but at Paul's own expense (vss. 33-35). In making this last point, Paul quotes a saying of Jesus that is preserved nowhere else. Paul did not have our written Gospels, but he had an authentic oral tradition about Jesus. He certainly was not as ignorant concerning Jesus' earthly life and teaching as some have supposed.

The second theme is a solemn announcement that he will never see them again (vss. 22-25). He is going to Jerusalem, "bound in the Spirit." So he expresses his overwhelming sense that he must go there to fulfill the purpose of God. Years earlier, Jesus had set his face to go to Jerusalem with much the same grim determination (see Luke 9:51). Already the Holy Spirit had warned Paul, probably through the prophets who were found in every church, that imprisonment and affliction awaited him there. But he must go on, even at the cost of his life. The gift from the Gentiles to the Jerusalem church had become for Paul an indispensable testimony to the grace of God. His ministry could not be complete without it.

The third theme is a solemn charge to the elders to do their duty (vss. 28-32). First they must take heed to themselves. Only as their own actions were upright, only as their own spiritual life ran true and deep, could they carry out the second part of their duty: to take heed to the flock, to feed the Church of the Lord. Two strong motivations are provided along with this command.

Though they had probably been elected by the people, they were to remember that it was ultimately the Holy Spirit himself who had made them officers. And they were to remember that the flock, the Church, which was placed in their charge, was so precious to Christ that he shed his own blood to obtain it. Paul warns them of the enemies from without and within who will seek to destroy the Church after he is gone (vss. 29-30). And he commends them to God, who alone can make them strong enough to win the victory (vs. 32).

What a tender parting followed! They knelt for prayer, they wept, they embraced, they escorted him to the ship. Paul was not only a great theologian and a great preacher; he was a great pastor. Only a man with a pastor's heart receives such devotion and affection from his people.

The Visit to Tyre (21:1-6)

We return to the log of Paul's travels. From Miletus the ship skirted the coast of Asia Minor to Patara. There Paul and his companions changed ships, finding one sailing directly for Tyre to unload cargo there. Tyre had been a great city when the Phoenicians were the leading traders of the Mediterranean (see Ezek. 26:1—28:19). It was still an important port. There Paul found a Christian church, doubtless founded by refugees from the persecution that arose over Stephen (see 11:19). He spent a week there, and once again men inspired by the Spirit warned Paul not to go to Jerusalem. The scene in verse 5 is one of the most beautiful in Acts: the blue waves of the Mediterranean, the sandy beach, the sailing vessel unloaded and ready to pull up anchor, the little band of Christians with wives and little children kneeling about Paul and his companions in a farewell prayer. Here is a one-sentence painting of "the fellowship" (see the comment on Acts 2:41-42).

The Visit to Caesarea (21:7-14)

The ship went on to Ptolemais, where they visited the brethren briefly. From there, either by sea or land, they came to Caesarea (see the comment on 10:1-33). Philip, one of the original seven, had settled there years before (see 8:40). Now he became Paul's host. Prophecy (see the comment on 11:27-30) was particularly strong at Caesarea. Four of Philip's daughters had this gift, an indication of the active participation of women in the Early

Church. Soon Agabus came down (see 11:27-30). He performed
a symbolic action, reminiscent of the Old Testament prophets
(compare Isa. 20; Jer. 27; Ezek. 4). Taking Paul's girdle, he
bound his own feet and hands. He predicted that the Jews at Jerusalem would so bind Paul and deliver him to the Gentiles. This
was the climax of all the warnings Paul had received. Even his
companions joined in begging him not to go further. He was
deeply touched by this, but still determined to complete his mission, even at the possible cost of his life. Seeing this, his companions resigned themselves to the will of God.

Paul Is Made a Prisoner (21:15—23:35)

Paul Arrives in Jerusalem (21:15-16)

Pentecost was now close at hand. The little band of representa-
tives from the churches of the Gentiles gathered their belongings
and set out for Jerusalem. Christians from Caesarea accompanied
them. Either on the way to Jerusalem or in Jerusalem itself, they
stayed with a disciple who had been a member of the Church
from its very beginning, one Mnason of Cyprus. It may be that
Luke learned from him some of the stories recounted in Acts 1
through 12.

Paul Attempts to Pacify the Jerusalem Church (21:17-26)

The day after his arrival, Paul officially reported to the Jerusalem church. James (see the comment on 12:6-17) and the
elders (see the comment on 11:27-30) received him. Doubtless
he delivered at this time the gift from the Gentile churches,
though Luke does not mention it (but see 24:17). He made a
full report of what God had done through him among the Gentiles, which James and the elders received with joy. Then they
reported to him on the state of the Jerusalem church. There were
at that time many thousands of Jewish Christians. They believed
in Jesus as the promised Messiah, yet they continued faithfully to
observe the Law of Moses. For them Christianity was still a sect
within Judaism.

These Jewish Christians were highly suspicious of Paul. Most
of Paul's churches were built around a nucleus of Jews, who had
been converted under his preaching in the synagogues (see 13:43;
14:1; 17:4, 11-12; 18:4; 19:9). James and his group felt that
these Jews should continue to observe the Jewish law and cus-

toms, as the Jerusalem church did. They suspected Paul of granting Jewish Christians the same freedom that the Gentiles had been given. We can hardly doubt, if we read Paul's letters, that their suspicions were correct. Though he himself continued to observe Jewish customs, he was convinced that the Law was no longer binding on a Christian—whether he were Jewish or Gentile (see Gal. 2:11-21; 3:23-29; 4:21-31; 5:4; Rom. 3:21-31; 7:4-6).

James and the elders proposed that Paul should demonstrate to the Jerusalem church that he was not teaching Jews to forsake Moses. Four of the Jerusalem Christians had taken a Nazirite vow (see the comment on 18:18-23). Let Paul join with them and pay the expenses involved in their purification ceremony. Paul agreed to do so.

Did he thus compromise the principle that he urges so vehemently in his letters—that Christ has freed us from the Law? Paul clearly believed that a Christian could refrain from the use of his freedom for the sake of a weaker brother's conscience, without surrendering freedom in principle (see Rom. 14:12-23; I Cor. 8). He was willing to become "as one under the law" in order to "win those under the law" (see I Cor. 9:19-23). He had previously taken a Nazirite vow himself (see 18:18). Yet this action would be interpreted by the Jerusalem church as a confession on his part that the Law was still binding on Jewish Christians. Paul clearly did not believe that. It is difficult to see how he agreed to go along with James. Did his ardent desire for the unity of the Church override all else at this point?

The compromise did not succeed. When Paul was arrested there is no indication that his fellow Christians in Jerusalem raised a finger to help him. The New Testament gives us no further view of the great Jewish wing of Christianity. About ten years after this, the Jews launched a disastrous rebellion against Rome, and in A.D. 70 Jerusalem was destroyed. Many of the Jewish Christians fled to Pella, but there was never a strong Jewish church after that. From A.D. 70 to the present, Christianity has been largely a Gentile movement.

Paul Is Mobbed and Arrested (21:27-40)

The purification took seven days, indicating that the four Jerusalem Christians had probably come in contact with a dead body (see Num. 6:9-12). When the seven days were almost completed,

Paul was attacked by Jews from Asia. These were evidently not Jewish Christians but the same Jews who were stubborn and disbelieved when Paul preached in the synagogue at Ephesus (see 19:9). They had plotted against him before (see 20:19). Now they seized him in the Temple, accusing him in general of teaching "against . . . the law and this place" (compare the charge against Stephen in 6:13); and in particular of bringing Trophimus the Ephesian into the inner part of the Temple, where all Gentiles were forbidden to go on pain of death.

The alarm spread through the city, swollen with pilgrims who had come to the Feast of Pentecost. Immediately a violent mob gathered. They dragged Paul out of the inner Temple, and the Temple officials ordered the gates shut to prevent further violence there. Word reached the tribune in charge of Roman forces in Jerusalem. He alerted at least two "centuries," each of about one hundred men and commanded by a centurion. Assuming personal command, he came at a run from his headquarters in the Tower of Antonia, which afforded a clear view of the Temple enclosure and was connected with it by two flights of steps.

This prompt action saved Paul's life, for he was about to be beaten to death by the furious mob. The tribune immediately arrested Paul, considering him the main cause of the disorder. It was impossible to find out the facts amid the shouting rioters, so Paul had to be taken to the barracks. The soldiers had to carry him bodily up the stairs to keep the crowd from killing him.

At the entrance to the Tower of Antonia, Paul was for the first time able to speak to the tribune. The tribune was amazed that he spoke Greek. From the wild cries of the crowd, he had gathered that Paul was an Egyptian revolutionary, who had raised a guerrilla army of Sicarii, or "dagger-men." Josephus records a similar story. Paul identified himself as a Jew, therefore in the Temple by right; and a native of Tarsus, therefore naturally able to speak Greek. He obtained permission to address the people, and when they grew quiet, he began to speak in Aramaic. This language, kin to the ancient Hebrew of the Scriptures, was much more acceptable to a Jerusalem crowd than Greek.

Paul's Defense to the Jews (22:1-21)

This is one of the most dramatic scenes in Acts. Paul stands at the top of the stairs leading to the Tower, disheveled from being beaten, bound with two chains. Below him the open courtyard of the Temple area is filled with Jews, with angry faces but strangely hushed by hearing Paul use Aramaic.

Paul's defense is a simple telling of the story of his life. Luke introduces in this way facts about the early life of Paul we had not known before: he was born at Tarsus; he was a pupil of Gamaliel. Beginning with verse 4, the story closely parallels what Luke has already recorded in Acts 9. There is not, however, the word-for-word repetition we find sometimes when stories are retold. Variations include: the new detail that Paul's conversion took place about noon (vs. 6); the apparent contradiction that his companions saw the light and did not hear the voice (vs. 9; compare 9:7); and a commission given him by Ananias (vss. 14 and 15).

The incident in verses 17-21 has not been related before at all. During the period in Jerusalem described in 9:26-30, Paul, as he prayed in the Temple, had a vision of Christ. In the vision, the Lord warned him to leave Jerusalem because the Jews would never accept his testimony. Paul protested that the Jews should not doubt him, since he had been a persecutor of the Church. But the Lord ordered him to leave and go to the Gentiles (22:21).

Paul Asserts His Citizenship (22:22-29)

The very word "Gentiles" set the Jews in a frenzy again. They shouted; they waved their garments; they threw dust into the air. The tribune was alarmed and puzzled. Either he could not understand Aramaic, and so did not know what Paul had said; or he did not understand the Jews, and so could not explain the new outbreak of rioting over Paul's simple story. He determined to get to the bottom of the matter and ordered Paul to be examined by scourging. This meant he would be beaten with whips until he was ready to tell the whole truth.

One of the centurions was directing this when Paul asked him if it were lawful to scourge a Roman citizen who had not yet been found guilty of anything. Of course it was not (see the comment on 16:35-40). The centurion ran in alarm to the tribune, who came immediately. It is interesting that we have no knowledge of how Roman citizenship was proved. Did citizens carry an official paper? At any rate, the tribune knew Paul was telling the truth. He began to converse with him as with an equal. He told Paul that he had bought citizenship for a large sum. Paul proudly replied: "I was born a citizen." This means that Paul's father was a citizen. Citizenship may have been his by purchase, or conferred as a reward for some special favor rendered to the emperor.

No scourging took place. All those who had had anything to do with Paul's arrest and examination were frightened. Paul remained a prisoner, but he could not be punished until he had been tried.

Paul Before the Sanhedrin (22:30—23:10)

On the next day, the tribune carried Paul before the Sanhedrin. When Paul protested his innocence, the high priest ordered him struck on the mouth. Caiaphas was no longer high priest; the years had seen many different high priests since Peter and John stood before the Sanhedrin (see 4:6). Now the office was held by Ananias. This is the third Ananias in Acts (see 5:1-5 and 9:10-17); they are three different men. Paul, unaware that Ananias held this high office, blazed in natural anger against his unlawful command, calling him a whitewashed wall. He later apologized for this outbreak.

Before any real investigation could be made, Paul succeeded in throwing the court into utter confusion. The high-priestly family were all members of the Sadducee party. In most of the affairs of Jerusalem, their control was unquestioned. But whenever the full Sanhedrin, in which a number of Pharisees held seats, had to be assembled, the Sadducees were on shaky ground. Once before, we have seen a Pharisee thwart their purposes (see 5:33-39). Paul took advantage of this natural division in the Sanhedrin by crying out, "I am a Pharisee," and by declaring that the real issue in his case was the resurrection of the dead. This was the sorest doctrinal difference between Pharisees and Sadducees. The dissension that followed grew so violent that the investigation had to be called off and soldiers had to rescue Paul and carry him back to the barracks.

There are two possible interpretations of this episode. One is that the tribune actually wanted to dispose of Paul's case by having him tried by the Sanhedrin. The other is that he merely carried him before the Sanhedrin to gather more information about the case, intending to turn Paul over to the Roman procurator when next he visited Jerusalem. In either case, he failed. Nothing was to be learned or decided by the riotous outcome of Paul's visit to the Sanhedrin.

An Encouraging Vision (23:11)

Paul was definitely the "charismatic type" (see the comment on 13:1-3). Again and again at crucial points in his life, he saw visions (see 9:3-9; 22:17-21; 16:9; 18:9). These experiences were very real to Paul, and he never doubted that God spoke to him through them. In modern times we tend to dismiss all such things as mere emotionalism, but Paul stands as proof that a visionary temperament and a critical intelligence can belong to the same man. In this vision, Jesus assured him that his arrest was not the end of his chance to go to Rome, as it seemed to be. Not in the way he had planned, but nevertheless surely, Paul would bear his witness at Rome.

The Plot to Ambush Paul (23:12-22)

Lawlessness was increasing in Jerusalem at this period. Josephus tells of bands of "Sicarii" (dagger-men) who roved the city and murdered in broad daylight. Four thousand of them had joined in an abortive revolt led by "the Egyptian" (see 21:38). It was perhaps some of these men who bound themselves by an oath neither to eat nor to drink till they had killed Paul. They asked the Sanhedrin to request a further hearing, and planned to ambush Paul between the Tower of Antonia and the Council Chamber.

At this point we learn something else about Paul we had not known before: he apparently had a married sister living in Jerusalem. Her son, Paul's nephew, was at this time a young man, probably in his twenties. In some way he learned of the plot. He went to the barracks and was permitted to speak to Paul, an indication that Paul was treated as an honorable prisoner. Paul then called one of the centurions and had his nephew taken to the tribune himself, to whom the plot was reported fully.

Paul Sent to Caesarea (23:23-35)

The tribune was a man of decisive action. He ordered out a large force of men, commanded by two centurions, to escort Paul to Felix, the procurator, whose headquarters were in Caesarea. To reduce the danger of riot, he resolved to move Paul by night. He sent a letter of explanation with the prisoner.

The letter reveals several interesting things. The tribune's name indicates that he was a Greek freedman, who was freed during the reign of the Emperor Claudius. As officials have done everywhere and at all times, he omits any reference to his mistakes, and presents his actions in the best possible light. He was, however, sincerely convinced that Paul was innocent of any offense against Roman law.

The large body of foot soldiers marched as far as Antipatris and returned. The horsemen went on and delivered Paul safely to Felix. After preliminary questioning, Felix put Paul under guard in a palace which Herod the Great had built and which the Roman procurators used as their headquarters. There he awaited his accusers.

Paul Before Felix (24:1-27)

Felix

When Herod Agrippa died (see 12:18-23), the direct rule of Roman governors or procurators over Judea and Samaria was resumed. From about A.D. 48 to 52, the governor was Cumanus. Under him, in a subordinate post in Samaria, was a freedman named Felix. Felix and his brother Pallas had been slaves of Antonia, the mother of the Emperor Claudius. They became personal favorites of Claudius. When Cumanus was retired in disgrace, Claudius promoted Felix to take his place. Never before had a freedman held such a high post. Felix sought to improve his position by marrying Drusilla, the daughter of Herod Agrippa. But the Jews hated him, and his reign was marked by lawlessness and revolts. When Claudius, his protector, died and Nero became emperor, Felix was replaced. It seems impossible to determine whether this was after some years (around A.D. 59) or almost immediately (around A.D. 56). Tacitus, the Roman historian, says Felix exercised the power of a king with the heart of a slave. Before this man Paul was now to be tried.

Tertullus Brings Charges (24:1-9)

After five days the accusers arrived. The original plaintiffs had been Jews of Asia, but the high priest himself now preferred charges. Tertullus was retained as the plaintiffs' attorney. He was probably a Hellenistic Jew whose fluent Greek would be pleasing to Felix.

Tertullus begins by praising the governor. Peace and reforms were not marks of Felix's rule, but rather the opposite. A freedman was hardly entitled to be called "most excellent." But Tertullus is a shameless flatterer. Finally he gets to the accusation. (1) Paul is generally defamed as a pestilent fellow, an agitator, a ringleader of the sect of the Nazarenes. Here is another Jewish name for Christianity (compare "the Way" in 9:1-9). (2) He is specifically accused of trying to profane the Temple. The best manuscripts do not include the point that the Jews would have settled the case if Lysias had not interfered (see margin), but Tertullus may well have said something of this kind.

Paul Defends Himself (24:10-21)

Paul, by contrast, does not flatter Felix, but simply states the fact that Felix has been in Palestine long enough to understand a case of this kind. He admits that he had gone up to worship at Jerusalem, but denies engaging in any arguments or disputes. He admits that he does belong to a special group, preferring to call it "the Way" rather than "the Nazarenes." He maintains, however, that this so-called "sect" is completely true to the Old Testament, especially in the matter of the resurrection of the dead. We can see Ananias gritting his teeth at that! Paul goes on to say that his conscience is clear. He begins the story of his arrest in the Temple, but breaks off to point out that the Jews of Asia were the real accusers on that occasion and should be at the trial. The only thing for which the high priest and his party can legally accuse him is his remarks about the resurrection before the Sanhedrin.

Felix Procrastinates (24:22-27)

Felix never rendered a decision in Paul's case. He was interested in "the Way," and found Paul an entertaining prisoner to keep around. First he told the Jews he would not decide the case until Lysias the tribune came. There is no record that he ever came or that Felix ever interviewed him. Paul was kept in custody, but his friends came and went freely. From time to time, Felix and Drusilla sent for Paul and asked him to discuss the Christian faith. Paul preached to them along the lines of his sermons to Gentiles in 14:15-17 and 17:22-31: "about justice and self-control and future judgment." Felix was alarmed but not converted. He hoped to be bribed by Paul. Instead, he may have been bribed by the Jews. For when he was succeeded by Festus, he did not cancel all pending cases as was often done, but left Paul in custody as "a favor" to the Jews.

A famous problem in this passage is the meaning of the words "when two years had elapsed" in verse 27. This may mean that Felix kept Paul in custody for two years. Or it may mean that Felix was procurator for only two years. Only the new discovery of inscriptions or records can settle this, and until this point is settled we cannot estimate accurately the date of Paul's arrival at Rome. Even if Paul was held less than two years by Felix, his stay at Caesarea was a considerable one. It is possible that some of the "Prison Epistles" were written there, rather than at Ephesus or Rome.

Paul Before Festus (25:1-12)

The Jews Reopen the Case (25:1-5)

Felix was replaced by Porcius Festus. Very little is known of him. He made a great effort to restore order in Palestine, but died after holding office a short time.

When Festus first arrived in his province, he went straight to Jerusalem, realizing that the center of his problem was there. The chief priests and their party immediately reopened the case against Paul. They petitioned that he be brought to Jerusalem. From 25:15, it would seem that they wanted him brought there for sentencing, without any further trial. But their main design was to ambush Paul on the way. Festus, with typical Roman prudence, suggested that Paul's accusers accompany him to Caesarea and open the hearings there.

Paul Appeals to Caesar (25:6-12)

The case was reopened before the Roman tribunal at Caesarea. Many accusations were made, which Luke does not give in detail. Paul defended himself—at length, we may believe—though Luke gives the briefest possible summary. Festus asked Paul if he were willing to go to Jerusalem for trial. The words "before me" suggest that Festus intended to be the judge.

But Paul's reply indicates that he understood the proposal otherwise. To be tried in Jerusalem would, for him, remove the case from Roman jurisdiction and place him in the authority of the Jews. This is surely what he means by "give me up to them" in verse 11. Paul was sure that his chances under Roman law were far better. So he took a resolute stand. Festus was Caesar's representative; his court was Caesar's tribunal. This was the proper place for a Roman citizen to be tried. If Festus would not try him there, let him be sent to Caesar himself for trial.

Unfortunately, we do not know just what the Roman law was concerning an appeal to Caesar. The word "appeal" may be misleading to modern ears. Paul was not appealing from the decision of a lower court, for no decision had been rendered. He was asserting his right to be heard by Caesar himself in Rome. It is probable that any Roman citizen could ask for such a trial. It was not automatically granted. Festus consulted with his council, and apparently could have refused. But it presented him an easy way out. To acquit Paul would have angered the Jews at the outset of his rule. To condemn him was hardly possible under Roman law. To send him to Caesar was a perfect answer.

Paul Before Agrippa (25:13—26:32)

Herod Agrippa II and Bernice

Herod Agrippa I (see the comment on 12:1-5) left several children at his death. Drusilla (see 24:24), the youngest, was only six years old; Agrippa II, the oldest, was seventeen. The Romans considered the latter too young to rule his father's kingdom, and he never became king of Judea. By the time of Paul's arrest, however, he had become king of the territory in the northeast which Philip had ruled (see Luke 3:1). He also was given by the Romans the custody of the sacred vestments of the high priest, which actually meant he had the power to remove and appoint high priests. He was, in a sense, the titular head of the Jewish church.

Bernice was his sister, another daughter of Herod Agrippa I. She was one of the most notorious women of the ancient world. She had been married to her uncle, Herod of Chalcis. She later married Polemon of Cilicia, and later still became the mistress of the Emperor Titus. Her close relationship with her own brother was a constant scandal.

Agrippa Agrees to Hear Paul (25:13-22)

Agrippa and Bernice came to pay an official welcome visit to the new governor. Festus was delighted. He had to prepare a written account of Paul's case to accompany him to Rome, and he was thoroughly mystified by the charges of the Jews. The titular head of the Jewish church could certainly help him here.

Festus described the case to Agrippa. It is interesting to see how the religious conflict between Paul and the Jews appeared to an intelligent Roman. It was a dispute about "their own superstition." But he had not missed the most essential point: it was about "one Jesus, who was dead, but whom Paul asserted to be alive." Agrippa readily agreed to hear Paul himself.

The Defense Before Agrippa (25:23—26:23)

This is the last major speech in Acts, and Luke intends it to be the climax. He carefully paints the scene. The great audience hall of Herod's praetorium (see 23:35) is decorated for a state occasion. Agrippa and Bernice enter with great pomp, followed by a long train of army officers and prominent local citizens. Festus barks a command and the soldiers lead Paul in. Festus then makes a formal speech to Agrippa in which, for the benefit of the large audience, he once again reviews Paul's case. He makes it clear that the purpose of this hearing is to gather information for the paper he must send with Paul to Caesar.

Agrippa gives Paul permission to speak, and the great address begins. After a courteous opening, in which Paul compliments Agrippa on his knowledge of Jewish affairs, Paul begins the story of his life. He speaks of his strict upbringing as a Jew and a Pharisee, and declares that the real issue in his trial is the hope of the resurrection of the dead. He recalls his persecution of the followers of Jesus of Nazareth and admits that he actually voted for, or strongly approved, the death of Stephen.

Then he tells once again the story of his conversion. It is not identical with the account in 9:1-19 or with the one in 22:6-16. In this speech the whole party is said to have fallen to the ground. And here it is specified that Jesus spoke to Paul in Aramaic. And here the words, "It hurts you to kick against the goads," are included. This must refer to the goads of Paul's own conscience, haunted as he was by the face of Stephen. The most striking difference is that Ananias drops out of the story entirely, and Paul receives his commission directly from the mouth of the Risen Lord. The commission includes a definite mission to the Gentiles. As we have seen, Paul's mission to the Gentiles slowly unfolded before him as he was led by the Spirit. But it is not uncommon for a man, in looking back, to see far more in his original call than he was aware of at the time.

Paul recognizes that the mission to the Gentiles is such a de-

parture from normal Jewish custom that it demands an explanation. The point of every speech he has made since his arrest is
that he has done this in obedience to a heavenly vision. In verse
20 he summarizes what he has preached to Jews and Gentiles
alike: Repent, turn to God, and perform deeds worthy of your
repentance. This is a thoroughly Jewish message and sounds like
John the Baptist. It is for this, says Paul, that the Jews seized me
and tried to kill me.

In verses 22-23 he moves on to a more distinctly Christian
message: The Scriptures have been fulfilled; the Messiah has suffered and has risen from the dead; he proclaims light both to
Jews and to Gentiles. This is strikingly like the summary of the
teaching of the Risen Lord in Luke 24:44-47.

Paul Seeks to Convert Agrippa (26:24-29)

Paul was interrupted, as often happened. Festus, forgetting his
dignity, cried out with a loud voice: "Paul, you are mad; your
great learning is turning you mad." It is interesting that Paul,
despite the strangeness of his "superstition" (25:19), had im-
pressed Festus as a man of great learning. Paul denied the charge
of insanity, but claimed inspiration. The Greek word translated
"I am speaking" in verse 25 is the word for inspired utterance
found in 2:4. He called on Agrippa to confirm the fact that he
was speaking sober truth. A governor newly come from Rome
might be ignorant of these things, but Agrippa had surely heard
that a growing band of the followers of one Jesus claimed everywhere that he had been raised from the dead. He had probably
heard of Paul, the great persecutor of "the Way," who suddenly
became its great champion. By now there were communities of
these people in almost every city, contemptuously called "Christians" by their neighbors. Paul properly used a familiar proverb:
"This was not done in a corner."

Now comes the most amazing part of the whole scene. The
man who was called in to be questioned begins to question. Paul
makes a direct appeal to Agrippa. "King Agrippa, do you believe
the prophets? I know that you believe." Paul must have intended
to start with some of the passages in the prophets and prove, as
he so often did, "that the Christ was Jesus" (see 9:22; 17:3;
18:5). But Agrippa cuts him short with a sarcastic remark that
reveals both his knowledge of "the Way" (he uses the word
"Christian") and his contempt for it. Some translators and inter-

preters have taken Agrippa's words as a sincere confession that he is almost ready to become a Christian. This does not fit the scene here, nor what we know of the rest of Agrippa's life. His real meaning must have been: "You surely think you can make a Christian of me in a hurry!" Paul replies most courteously and earnestly that, hurry or no, he wishes he could. In a dramatic gesture, he calls attention to his chains and says, "Would to God that not only you but also all who hear me this day might become such as I am—except for these chains."

The Appeal to Caesar Holds (26:30-32)

The hearing abruptly adjourned. Festus conferred with Agrippa, Bernice, and his council. The general consensus was that Paul was innocent of all charges. Agrippa told Festus that Paul could have been freed if he had not appealed to Caesar. Apparently Festus felt that the case was entirely out of his hands. As he had no right to condemn a man who had appealed to Caesar, neither did he have the right to acquit him. The Caesar to whom Paul was now to be sent was Nero.

The Journey to Rome (27:1—28:31)

The Voyage to Fair Havens (27:1-8)

Festus was apparently convinced that the hearing before Agrippa had yielded all the light on Paul's case he was apt to get, so he moved immediately to send Paul to Rome. Paul, with some other prisoners, was delivered to a centurion named Julius. It has been suggested that the Augustan Cohort, to which Julius was attached, was a special courier service, responsible directly to the emperor. But inscriptions show that there was an auxiliary cohort, composed mainly of Syrian troops, which bore that name and which was stationed in Palestine in the first century.

The "we" reappears in 27:1 for the first time since Paul reached Jerusalem in 21:17. Where had Luke been in the interval? There is no indication. It is a reasonable guess that he had not left Paul at all. He was perhaps one of the friends who attended to his needs during the imprisonment at Caesarea (see 24:23). He may have spent the time there gathering material for the account of Jesus' life he planned to write. From Caesarea he would have had easy access to many of those "who from the beginning were eyewitnesses and ministers of the word" (see Luke

1:2). For reasons known only to himself, our author uses "we" only when there is rapid movement from place to place. He never uses it when telling of a prolonged stay in one place. Thus it drops out soon after the arrival at Philippi (see 16:17), soon after the arrival at Jerusalem (see 21:17), and soon after the arrival at Rome (see 28:16).

Another interesting question is: How were Luke and Aristarchus (see vs. 2; compare the comment on 20:1-6) permitted to accompany a prisoner to Rome? If Paul had been a condemned prisoner, this probably would not have been permitted. But no decision had ever been given; he was simply being held pending a trial. And the fact that he was to be tried by Caesar himself gave him certain prestige. It must have seemed reasonable, then, to Festus and to Julius, to let Paul's companions go along. This would be all the more likely if Paul needed medical care from Luke, a physician. It is hardly necessary to suppose, as some commentators do, that Luke and Aristarchus had to pose as Paul's slaves. Paul may have had to pay their expenses; perhaps he had to pay his own, too; we do not know.

Julius embarked with his company in a ship whose home port was Adramyttium, a city not far from Troas, on the west coast of the Province of Asia. This was apparently a small vessel which would work its way from harbor to harbor along the coast until it reached home. The first stop was at Sidon in Phoenicia (see 11:19), where Paul was permitted to visit friends. Already it was growing too late in the year for good sailing, so the captain of the ship did not dare sail straight across to Asia. He took the long way around, under the lee of Cyprus and along the coast of Cilicia and Pamphylia. Finally they reached Myra, an important port on the southern coast of Asia, in what had been the ancient kingdom of Lycia.

At Myra, Julius found a ship of Alexandria, bound for Italy. Egyptian grain was the staple diet of Rome, and its uninterrupted transportation was so important to the life of the city that the government itself owned and operated a fleet of grain ships. It was probably to such a ship that Julius now transferred his company. It would be a larger ship, prepared to sail across the open sea direct to Italy. The winds, however, were so contrary that even this ship could scarcely creep along the coast to Cnidus. From there they attempted to cross to Sicily, but were blown south and had to run before the wind until the island of Crete offered refuge. They reached a small harbor known as Fair Havens.

Paul Warns Against Sailing (27:9-12)

By this time "the fast" was already past. This refers to the Jewish Day of Atonement, which fell in late September or early October. September and October were considered risky months for sailing; all navigation ceased by November. A council was held by the centurion and the captain and the owner of the ship. The "owner" was probably not a private merchant, but operated the ship and supervised the cargo on concession from the government. Paul must have already made a profound impression on these men, for, although a prisoner, he was admitted to their consultation and asked to give his advice.

As a prophet (see 13:1 and the comment on 11:27-30), Paul predicted that if the ship left the harbor, there would be great injury and loss of cargo, ship, and lives. But Fair Havens was a poor harbor for wintering; and scarcely one hundred miles west, on the coast of Crete, was Phoenix, a much better harbor. So the majority voted to move on to Phoenix.

The Storm Strikes (27:13-20)

A gentle south wind sprang up—just what they needed in order to sail close along the shore of Crete. So they weighed anchor. Suddenly, without warning, howling down from the seven-thousand-foot peaks of Crete, the dread northeaster struck, driving the ship to the southwest, away from the land. There was no way to get back to Crete. Luke describes their desperate efforts to save themselves in first-century seaman's language, and often we can only guess what he means.

First, as they ran under the lee of a small island named Cauda, or Clauda, they managed to hoist aboard the longboat, which had apparently been tied behind the ship (vss. 16-17). Next, they "used helps to undergird the ship" (see vs. 17, margin). This probably refers to a long cable which was run along the deck from one end of the ship to the other. Supports, or "helps," were set up down the center of the deck. As they were raised, they drew the cable tighter and tighter. Such cables are found in pictures of Egyptian ships, though not of Roman and Greek ships. This ship was from Alexandria. The purpose of "undergirding" was to keep the ship from "hogging" or breaking in two in the center. That would be the great danger if the ship should run

upon the Syrtis, the treacherous sandbanks off the north coast of
Africa. Next they "lowered the gear." We do not know whether
this means that they unfurled the sails from the yardarms and so
tried to run out the storm under full sail, or that they took down
all the sails and let the wind drive the ship where it would, or that
they lowered a drag-anchor.

On the second day, when there was no letup in the storm, they
began to throw things overboard. This was not the main cargo of
wheat (see vs. 38), but something else. On the third day, they
threw out the tackle, probably all the spare ropes and sails. The
storm raged on, with the sky so overcast that they could not determine their position from sun or stars. After days of this, all
hope was lost.

Paul Predicts Deliverance (27:21-26)

In this time of despair and hunger—for they had been unwill-
ing or unable to eat—Paul came forward. He could not resist the
common human pleasure of saying, "I told you so." But his main
purpose was to correct the prophecy he had made earlier (see vs.
10). Then he had been sure that all would be lost. But now, as
the result of a vision (see the comment on 23:11), he was sure
no lives would be lost, but only the ship.

Long before, Paul had made Rome his goal (see 19:21).
Again and again it seemed impossible that he would ever get there.
Delivering the offering to Jerusalem took him out of his way. He
was delayed en route. When he finally arrived in Jerusalem, his
arrest seemed the end of all hope that he would get to Rome.
But in the barracks prison, the Lord had promised that he would
eventually "bear witness also at Rome" (see 23:11). In the
long months of imprisonment at Caesarea the promise seemed
only a mockery. Then, unexpectedly, the way opened for him:
he appealed to Caesar! Soon he was on the way. But hope thus
renewed was soon turned to despair. The storm broke. Had God
brought him thus far only to abandon him to the sea? No; in
the midst of the storm the promise was renewed: Paul would yet
reach Rome. As a special sign of favor, God would also deliver
all of the men who were on the ship.

Escape to the Shore (27:27-44)

Fourteen days after the storm struck, the sailors thought they
heard breakers ahead, and successive soundings showed that they

were indeed nearing land. It was midnight, so they let out four anchors from the stern, keeping the ship headed toward the unseen shore. It was dangerous to proceed further until daylight. The sailors, however, lowered the boat (see vs. 16), pretending that they would lay out anchors from the bow. Paul saw at once that their real purpose was to try to get ashore, even in the dark. He warned the centurion that if the sailors deserted there would be no way to get the ship to shore. So the soldiers quickly cut the ropes that held the boat and let it go.

Just before dawn, Paul urged them all to take some food. They needed strength for the final crisis. He assured them again that no one would perish. Then in a ceremony which was surely not the Lord's Supper, yet strongly resembled it, Paul took bread, gave thanks to God, broke it, and began to eat. This simple demonstration of faith somehow broke the terrible tension, and all of the men aboard took some food. Luke remarks that there were two hundred seventy-six of them. Some manuscripts say "about seventy-six," but the larger number is quite possible for an Egyptian grain ship. Following the meal, the cargo of wheat was thrown into the sea, to lighten the ship as much as possible.

In full daylight they could see the land, but they had no idea what island it was. They planned to drive the ship into a small bay and up on the beach. The ship was apparently straining against the anchors toward the shore, so three things had to be done quickly and almost at once. The anchors were cast off; the ropes by which the rudder-oars had been hoisted into the ship for the night were loosened, dropping the rudders instantly into steering position; and the foresail was hoisted to catch the wind. The ship sprang forward and success seemed sure, when the ship suddenly struck "a place of two seas" (vs. 41, margin). This must mean a shoal or sand bar of some kind. The ship ran aground; its bow stuck fast; and the pounding surf began to break up the stern. The soldiers, whose own lives were at stake should prisoners escape, thought the safest plan would be to kill the prisoners outright. But Julius stopped them, for Paul's sake. Some swam ashore, and some floated on pieces of the wreckage. So, miraculously, all escaped to land.

This account of Paul's voyage and shipwreck is in many ways the finest piece of writing in Acts. The marks of an eyewitness are everywhere. The vocabulary is large, but not pretentious. The style is concise, direct, virile. The excitement never lags; the sus-

pense builds up to a tremendously satisfying climax. Students of
things nautical vouch for the accuracy of every sentence. In spite
of the many expressions we do not fully understand, more can
be learned here of how an ancient sailing vessel was handled
than from any other document of antiquity. But Luke's primary
purpose in this story is neither to entertain nor to give information about sailing ships. It is to show how God's purpose of bringing Paul to Rome could not be thwarted, and to set forth Paul
as an example of how a man of faith acts in apparently hopeless
circumstances.

Malta (28:1-10)

The island to which Paul and his companions had miraculously escaped turned out to be Melita, the modern Malta. It
was populated by descendants of the ancient Phoenicians. Luke
calls them "barbarians" ("natives"), meaning those who do not
speak Greek.

The people of Malta came to the aid of the weary, cold, half-
drowned survivors by building a large bonfire. In gathering a
bundle of sticks, Paul was bitten by a poisonous viper. The superstitious Maltese saw in this the hand of the goddess Dikē ("Justice"). Though this man had escaped the sea, he must still be
punished for some hidden crime. When no harm came to him,
they changed their minds and said he was a god. Some have
suggested that the promise, "they will pick up serpents," found
in the late ending of Mark (see Mark 16:18, margin), is based on
this incident.

Not far from where the ship had wrecked was the estate of
Publius, who was probably the ranking Roman official on the
island. When he learned of the refugees he brought them to his
home for three days. It is doubtful that he entertained the whole
crowd; probably the centurion and the captain and the owner
and Paul, with their attendants, were his guests. Paul was instru-
mental in healing Publius' father, who had fever and dysentery.
This news brought out all the sick on the island, and Paul had a
great healing ministry there.

Luke omits all else that happened on Malta. We do not know
where the party stayed after leaving Publius' house. We do not
know whether Paul founded a church on Malta. We do know
that the Maltese were grateful to him and loaded him down with
gifts when he departed.

Rome at Last (28:11-16)

Three months—probably November, December, and January —were spent on Malta. In February, navigation became possible again. Julius put his party aboard another Alexandrian grain ship, which had wintered in Malta. Luke recalls that it had a figurehead of Castor and Pollux, the twin gods who were special patrons of sailors. They sailed north to Syracuse, the great harbor on the island of Sicily. From there they continued north to Rhegium, on the tip of the Italian "boot." From Rhegium, a favorable wind enabled them to land at Puteoli, on the Bay of Naples, in just two days. There the heavy grain ships discharged their cargoes. The rest of the journey would be made by land.

At Puteoli there were "brethren"—Christians. This reminds us of the selectivity of Acts. Luke has not by any means told of the founding of all the churches. There were doubtless hundreds of towns like Puteoli, where there were Christian churches, founded by refugees and nameless missionaries. Peter and Paul did not do it all. What must it have meant to Paul, after his years of imprisonment and his months of peril at sea, to enjoy seven days of fellowship with these brethren!

Then began the trek to Rome itself. The last part of the journey was along the famous Appian Way. Here again Paul was met by brethren, from the church at Rome. They walked about forty-three miles to meet him. Paul thanked God and took courage. When they finally reached the city, Paul was doubtless handed over to the official who received such prisoners. He was assigned to light custody. He was permitted to live by himself, with only one soldier to guard him. Thus, though not in the way he had planned, Paul's desire to visit Rome was granted.

Paul and the Jews at Rome (28:17-28)

Paul began his ministry in Rome, as he had everywhere else, by preaching first to the Jews. He was not at liberty to go to the synagogue, so he called the Jewish leaders to his house. There was a large Jewish community at Rome, which played an active part in the city. Traces of at least nine synagogues have been found there. Claudius had tried to expel the Jews (see 18:2), but there were so many that he had not succeeded.

Paul had a personal reason for making contact with the Jewish leaders immediately. He was involved in the legal case, "The

Jews *vs.* Paul," to be tried before Caesar. He wanted to find out if his accusers had arrived in Rome. He knew that it was not likely the high priest himself would take the trouble to come to Rome. The high priest might save time and expense by asking the Jewish community in Rome to pursue the case for him.

This is why Paul starts out with a personal defense. He protests his innocence: he has done nothing against the people or the customs of the fathers. He relates briefly his arrest and the circumstances which forced him to appeal to Caesar. The Jews had often appealed to Caesar against the injustices of the Herods or the Roman governors. Paul may have been the first to appeal against his fellow Jews. So he hastens to add: "I had no charge to bring against my nation." To the contrary, it is because he is a true Israelite, loyal to the hope of Israel, that he is bound.

This defense proved unnecessary. No letters or messengers had been sent from Judea at all. But the Jewish leaders were eager to hear this rabbi, whose learning they could respect, expound the new faith. All they had heard of it had been hostile criticism.

The door was thus opened for Paul to preach the gospel to the Jews. He set a day, to give them time to assemble a crowd. At the appointed time a great number of them came to his lodging. All day long he tried to convince them, using Old Testament texts, as his custom was (see 13:16-41; 17:2-3, 11). Some were convinced, but others disbelieved. At the end there was a definite rupture. As at Pisidian Antioch (see 13:46-47), Corinth (see 18:6), and Ephesus (see 19:9), Paul turned to the Gentiles.

The turning at Rome is the most formal and final of all. Paul uses a long quotation from Isaiah. It is a most fitting one. Centuries before, the prophet Isaiah was deeply exercised because the people of Israel would not take his message to heart. It was revealed to him that the word of God is a two-edged sword. While it melts some hearts it hardens others. It leaves men better—or worse; more able to hear and understand—or less able. This great truth had been inherent in Isaiah's call to be a prophet (see Isa. 6:1-13). Jesus himself faced the same agonizing problem: why would not Israel hear him and understand? The words of Isaiah gave him an answer (see Matt. 13:14-15; Mark 4:12; Luke 8:10). Now Paul finds his answer in the same place. He follows the quotation with a ringing declaration: "Let it be known to you then that this salvation of God has been sent to the Gentiles; they will listen."

Two Years of Unhindered Ministry (28:30-31)

Luke ends Acts with a typical summary. Our eagerness to know what he does not tell should not draw our attention away from what he does tell. (1) Paul had two full years of ministry at Rome. In his long, eventful career the only places where he spent as much time were Antioch, Corinth, and Ephesus. Rome, then, was one of his major pastorates. (2) He lived at his own expense. Some of his churches sent gifts (see Phil. 4:18). But probably he was able to support himself as usual by tentmaking. We know that Roman prisoners were permitted to work. (3) Though he could not move about freely, many came to hear him. (4) The great themes of his preaching were the same: the Kingdom of God and the Lord Jesus Christ. These doctrines had a peculiar cutting edge in the city which was so conscious of the kingly power of Rome and the lordship of Caesar. (5) There was no serious opposition or hindrance to the gospel during the two-year period.

The End of Acts

Of course we want to know what happened after that. Luke has been interested in Paul's legal case and careful to point to each declaration of his innocence. If Paul was acquitted at Rome, why does he not tell that as his climax? If Paul was condemned and executed, it was certainly a miscarriage of justice. Why does Luke not say so, and glory in his martyrdom? If the case had not been settled when Luke wrote, why did he not wait for the settlement before issuing his book?

We can never really know the answers to these questions. It has been suggested that Luke wrote a third volume, which has been lost; or that he ran out of papyrus; or that the outcome was so well known he did not record it; or that he died before he finished writing. The most reasonable guess may be this: the case against Paul was simply dropped. His accusers, the Jews, never appeared; so there was no trial, no acquittal, no condemnation. We know that in cases appealed to the emperor, the accuser sometimes did not appear. After a reasonable time limit had expired, such cases were dropped. We have no official record of what that time limit was. It is not impossible that under Nero it was set at two years. Luke's readers would know this, and his statement that Paul was in Rome for two whole years would clearly mean that the time for a trial expired and he was then set at liberty.

For the rest of Paul's life we must rely on tradition. There is little reason to doubt that he was finally beheaded in Rome by Nero's orders after the changed attitude of Rome toward the Christians, following the Great Fire. Between the end of Acts and the end of Paul's life he may have made other journeys, even to Spain. Of these traditions we cannot be sure, though the "Pastoral Epistles" are strong evidence for a further period of missionary activity. Some students of Paul's life prefer the view that he was never released, but was executed after the end of the two years.

We must remember that Acts is not, after all, a biography of Paul. It is the story of what Jesus, through the Holy Spirit, continued to do in his Body, the Church. Luke's special emphasis is on the change-over from Jerusalem to Rome, from Christianity as a sect within Judaism to Christianity as an independent and largely Gentile religion. In a sense, with Paul's two years of ministry at Rome, Luke has finished that story.

In another sense the story is not yet finished. Jesus is still at work in his Church. And we who read this book are more than spectators at a drama. We are also actors on the stage.